FROM THE LIBRARY OF

ALICE STRAUGHAN

THE NO COOKING COOKBOOK

The NO COOKING *Cookbook*

BY LILLIAN LANGSETH-CHRISTENSEN

COWARD-McCANN, INC.

NEW YORK

In memory of my mother,
Ida Gaertner,
and her "golden hand."

Preface

I T SEEMS to me that any cookbook preface must talk about the subject in general rather than the particular book it sponsors.

So—it would be easy enough to mention only those rules, of thumb and memory, that the great chefs have passed on to us: Never use any but the finest ingredients; take care with the preparations; follow the recipe exactly; balance your meal for eye and taste appeal: if you are serving a vichysoisse first, then don't follow this with a cream sauce for the entrée and a custard for dessert. These are all good and very important rules, but surely there is more to it than that?

Yes, there is more. I know that for me, so long as I can prepare and serve the foods I like to people I like—then I have relaxed, and, I hope, helped those I love to do the same thing.

In the Viennese tradition followed in my family's kitchen, food was *very* important, for it implied all of the gaiety and warmth that came of good talk made better by meals that restored and wine that refreshed.

This is the wonderful thing about cooking, or, in this case, no cooking. It becomes a creation of one's own—to be given, yes, but to be shared as well between donor and recipient.

Few major wars, if any, have been fought over food. If one sticks strictly to recipes and overlooks the rich fields of wheat, the green and heavy pasture lands, then we may say there has never been a full-scale war fought over food. Small ones, yes. A recipe stolen has precipitated lifelong enmity; a snide criticism of a rival's skill has wound up in a chill dawn, the slanderer and the slandered having chosen pistols at twenty paces—for have we not said that food is important?

But by and large, food means sustenance, relief, enjoyment and, finally, love. One gives all of these things along with a fine dinner, a happy lunch. This is what the serving of food means to me, and a short time ago, when a friend talked of the drearily hot hours that lay ahead before she could serve a roast to her family, I thought immediately of all the good and common foods that wait only for a loving hand to make them distinctive and rare. This particular cooking book is the result. The recipes wait only for your hand.

—LILLIAN LANGSETH-CHRISTENSEN

Contents

The No Cooking Cookbook

THE NO COOKING COOKBOOK is a volume for everyone: the experienced cook and the novice. It does not attempt to replace the basic cookbooks on the kitchen shelf. Nor does it attempt to simplify, and perhaps spoil, recipes that demand complex preparation. Rather it presents the many attractive and tempting dishes that can be, and should be, made simply by combining several ingredients and serving them. Its keystone is imagination.

The concept of "Mix and Serve" has usually been applied to preparing alcoholic beverages and may explain why in our century of short cuts, drinking is so popular. If a Martini had to be boiled, reduced, clarified and simmered for eight hours . . . if it had to be marinated at room temperature over night, folded and chilled, molded, baked and unmolded, very few people would drink and no one would be foolhardy enough to give a cocktail party.

But the fact is, at a cocktail party or dinner "Mix and Serve" often applies just as appropriately to the food as to the drink. The world is full of wonderful combinations, eagerly waiting to be tried. The ease with which mix and serve recipes may be followed, the time and annoyance saved in following them and the assurance of unfailing success should all be regarded as bonuses.

Primarily the aim here is good eating. Try combining

1 basket strawberries
½ cup thin honey
½ cup chopped walnuts
Mix and Serve.

Elaborate instructions have been omitted. We are assuming that you will have no desire to eat the strawberry stems or the plastic basket and that you will not try to incorporate the honey jar or comb into the mixture.

Some of the combinations included in this volume—especially salads—will serve as main dishes. Most of them supplement the main dish. All these recipes assist in transforming your dinner from an everyday meal to a repast worthy of the most discriminating diners —members of your family or guests. And they do it in the simplest possible way, yielding a maximum eating pleasure in return for the minimum effort.

Here are more than 500 recipes for delicious sophisticated dishes that will add lustre to your menu. They will save time, effort, worry and expense. There are very few things left that will do that for anyone, let alone the cook.

The experienced cook will give a sigh of relief, the novice will give three cheers.

The NO COOKING COOKBOOK is not a cookbook in the accepted sense. It is a manual for everyone who cooks and who never has quite enough time. This is a book you may turn to when the chicken is boiling or the chops are broiling. It will give the reader a SOUP, a SALAD, a SAUCE and a DESSERT that only have to be mixed in order to be ready to serve and can be prepared while the main dish is roasting.

If you have time, bake your pie and roast your meat as usual, but relax about the appetizer and the vegetables—you'll find them in the NO COOKING COOKBOOK. You won't have to leaf through another cookbook or your memory for a short quick recipe. Just look in the freezer and take out a package of frozen peas. The NO COOKING COOKBOOK will do the rest.

If you are having meat loaf for dinner when unexpected guests arrive, these recipes will serve you well. They will help you to find the things to have before, with, and after the meat loaf, that will make it into a gala meal.

The NO COOKING COOKBOOK puts into a single volume all possible combinations that can be made without having to cook (or be one). You can go on for years without having to give hours for what will take minutes to eat. Just mix and serve out of the NO COOKING COOKBOOK.

NOTE: *All* recipes in this book will serve 4 to 6 people, except as otherwise specified.

HOW TO STIR Place ingredients into a bowl and move a spoon held upright, in widening circles from the center to the edge of the bowl, until all ingredients are well blended. It is a good rule to always stir in the same direction, although it is not always important.

HOW TO BEAT Place ingredients into a bowl and whip briskly with a large spoon or whisk, using a lifting motion. Beating should incorporate air into the mixture so it must always be done with a round motion that lifts the mixture as it beats. Do not overbeat.

HOW TO FOLD When adding a second ingredient to a stiffly beaten mixture, as whipped cream or stiff egg whites, it is important to fold the second ingredient into the first with a gentle folding motion, so that the air in the beaten mixture will not be lost. Use a spatula or large spoon, go down to the bottom of the bowl, then up to the surface in a wide circle always folding the beaten mixture over the second ingredient.

HOW TO CREAM BUTTER Let butter stand at room temperature until it is soft but not melted. Cream the soft butter in the electric beater or in a mixing bowl with a wooden spoon. Tilt the bowl so that the spoon can press the butter against the side of the bowl while creaming it. The butter will become light in color as well as in texture.

HOW TO CUBE, DICE, CHOP OR MINCE ONIONS (Beets, mushrooms, boiled potatoes, etc., are treated in the same way.) Place vegetables on a wooden chopping board and cut across into 1/4″ slices. Cut the slices into 1/4″ strips and cut across in the opposite direction into 1/4″ cubes. Increase or reduce the size of the cubes as the recipes require. In order to chop or mince the vegetable, spread the cubes out on the board, hold the tip of the knife in the left hand and the handle in the right hand and move up and down the board with a chopping motion until all the cubes are reduced to the size that is needed. If there is only a small quantity to chop, the vegetables may be chopped according to the directions for chopping parsley and herbs.

HOW TO CHOP PARSLEY (All herbs, shallots, scallions, garlic, nuts and olives should be chopped in this way.) Place parsley on a wooden chopping board, hold tip of a sharp knife firmly down on the board with the left hand. Hold the handle of the knife in the right hand and lift and lower it in a short chopping motion while moving back and forth in a fanlike arc across the parsley. The knife should pivot back and forth until the parsley is finely chopped or until it is finely minced. This method may be reversed by holding the knife handle in place and chopping back and forth with the tip of the knife. A mouli, food chopper or similar kitchen aid can be used for any of these purposes.

HOW TO PEEL A TOMATO   Dip tomato into boiling water for about forty seconds or while counting slowly to ten. Take tomato from water immediately and set aside to peel later or draw skin off at once by inserting a pointed knife under the fine outside skin and pulling it off in large pieces. If the skin does not come off easily, dip tomato into boiling water for a few more seconds. Unripe tomatoes do not peel as easily as ripe ones. Cool peeled tomatoes before serving but do not refrigerate a peeled tomato for more than an hour.

HOW TO BOIL WATER   This is the thing that some people say they cannot even do. Place fresh water in a clean saucepan, do not fill more than ¾ full. Cover saucepan and place over heat. When water reaches the boiling point, add salt, if the recipe requires.

HOW TO HARD-COOK AN EGG   Bring water to a boil in a saucepan that is large enough so that water will cover the egg. Add a little vinegar and dip a large spoon into the water. Place a room-temperature egg on the hot spoon and lower it carefully into the boiling water. Add remaining eggs. When water returns to a boil, lower the heat and stir the eggs in one direction for 1 minute. Cover eggs and boil 15 to 16 minutes longer. Pour off water and drop eggs into cold water making sure that the shell of each egg is broken. Let eggs cool, renewing the cold water if they have to cool quickly.

HOW TO PEEL A HARD-COOKED EGG   When hard-cooked eggs are cold, tap their entire surface gently with a spoon or knife in order to craze the shell. Start at the slight hollow at the wide end of the egg and draw off the broken shell in one piece.

HOW TO RICE A HARD-COOKED EGG   Separate hard-cooked egg white and yolk and press them separately through a coarse sieve. Use the back of a spoon to press them through the sieve.

HOW TO SEPARATE AN EGG   Use cold eggs, if possible, when separating them and then set them aside to reach room temperature before using them. Tap side of egg, at the center of the side, against the thin edge of a bowl or glass or cup. Do not tap against a thick edge as you will not get a sharp break and do not break with a knife as it often breaks the yolk. Hold the egg upright over a bowl, insert thumb nail and lift off top half of egg. The majority of the white will drop into the bowl and the yolk will remain in the lower half of the shell. (Always keep rounded end of egg at the bottom when breaking.) Transfer the yolk back and forth between the two half egg shells until all the white has drained down into the bowl. Another method is to break the egg as directed and after the majority of the white has flowed into the bowl, transfer the yolk into the palm of your hand and let the remaining white flow through your fingers. If this is your method, wash your hands between each egg. It is also a good idea to smell at each egg before adding it to the others in the bowl, just in case.

HOW TO BEAT EGGS   Beat room-temperature eggs in a bowl with a fork, rotary or electric beater until the whites and yolks are thoroughly incorporated and foamy.

HOW TO BEAT EGG YOLKS   Beat egg yolks at room temperature, in a bowl with a rotary or electric beater. They will become thick and pale lemon-colored. Egg yolks can be beaten with a fork or whisk, but as they should be as light and thick as possible a beater is recommended.

HOW TO BEAT EGG WHITES   Let egg whites come to room temperature, beat them in a deep bowl with a wire whisk, a rotary beater or an electric beater. It is best to use egg whites which are 2 to 4 days old for this purpose. The bowl should be small enough so that egg whites will be at least an inch deep in the bowl. Add a pinch of salt and beat until the whites are foamy and opaque but do not yet stand in soft peaks. If sugar is to be added to the recipe, start at this point and add it gradually while continuing to beat the eggs until they are stiff. If no sugar is to be added, continue to beat until stiff. The easiest way to gauge the proper stiffness is to invert the bowl or tilt it and if the eggs do not slide or move they are perfect.

HOW TO WHIP SOUR CREAM   Whip sour cream with a rotary beater or electric beater until it is light, creamy and smooth. It will not become stiff but it will increase slightly in volume.

HOW TO WHIP CREAM   Whip heavy, well chilled cream, which should be at least 24 hours old, in a chilled bowl with chilled beaters. For best results use a bowl which is small enough so that cream will be as deep as possible. Whip the cream with a wire whisk, a rotary beater or an electric beater. Beat rapidly while cream is liquid. As it gains in volume and becomes stiff, whip more slowly so that there will be no danger of overbeating. Cream should be light and soft; stop when it starts to look like a thunder cloud. Remember, cream separates suddenly when it is overbeaten and no one wants such expensive butter for dinner.

HOW TO WHIP A HALF CUP OF CREAM   Place chilled cream in a chilled cup and beat with a small wire whisk until it starts to thicken and expand. After that beat with a small electric hand beater or a small rotary beater.

HOW TO SCALD ALMONDS   Pour boiling water over shelled almonds and allow to steep for 4 to 5 minutes. Drain almonds, press them out of their skins and dry with a towel. Shelled pistachio nuts are scalded in the same way.

HOW TO SCALD HAZELNUTS (filberts)   Scald as almonds but increase steeping time to 8 to 10 minutes.

HOW TO DRY BREAD CRUMBS   Let bread which is to be used for crumbs dry out for 3 to 4 days. If it does not seem thoroughly dry, place it in a 200° F oven until it is crisp and brown. Crush the bread with a rolling pin and sift the crumbs through a sieve into a jar. Seal the jar and store in a cool dry place.

HOW TO GRATE HORSE RADISH   Peel a horse radish root, or a part of a root, and grate it against the side of a coarse metal grater. It is an easy process but usually irritates the eyes so that you will be forced to cry even more copiously than if you were grating onions. There is nothing that can be done to overcome this, except to buy grated horse radish. If you are using the bottled product, be sure to press it dry before using it. It is also important to cover freshly grated horse radish with a bowl to keep it from turning black immediately. It will turn in any case, so grate it just before serving (tears and all) if possible.

HOW TO CRUSH GARLIC   Use a small garlic press, placing one peeled garlic clove at a time in the press. Pull out the crushed skin before inserting the second clove. If a press is not available, peel the clove, mince it very finely with a knife or crush it in a mortar. The mortar, if it is wooden, will forever after smell slightly of garlic.

HOW TO MAKE GARLIC SALT   Stir 1 teaspoon salt with 1 crushed garlic clove, or mince the salt right with the garlic. If a mortar is used, crush the salt with the garlic. Always allow 1 teaspoon salt per garlic clove unless it is one of those large cloves, then increase the salt.

HOW TO JUICE AN ONION   Cut an onion across at the widest part and scrape the cut surface across with a spoon, so that only the juice is obtained.

HOW TO GRATE ORANGE AND LEMON PEEL   Wash and dry fruit, do not cut or peel it. Grate the whole fruit against the side of a metal grater, rotating the fruit so that only the colored rind is grated. As soon as the white membrane is exposed, turn the fruit. Use a knife or fork to scrape the grated rind from the grater. It is best to hold the grater over a piece of wax paper, rather than a bowl, so the gratings can be shaken together more easily.

HOW TO SLIVER ORANGE OR LEMON RIND   Wash and dry fruit and cut the thinnest possible layer from the outside rind of the fruit. Cut only the colored part of the rind. It is best to use a potato parer or a very sharp knife for this purpose. Turn the pieces of rind over on a chopping board, hold them firmly with the color side down, and scrape off any white membrane that adheres to the back. Cut the rind into the longest and thinnest possible slivers with a sharp knife.

HOW TO PRESS JUICE FROM ORANGES, LEMONS OR LIMES Cut fruit across, remove seeds and press in a juicer. If necessary it can be done with the hands, but requires considerable strength. If a juicer is used, do not press down so hard that the bitter white membrane will flavor the juice.

HOW TO MAKE VANILLA SUGAR Fold a fresh vanilla bean over several times, to break the surface, and bury it in a jar of powdered sugar. Always keep the jar closed when not in use. Refill the jar with sugar when necessary. The vanilla bean will last a long time before its strong flavor will fade.

HOW TO SCALD MILK AND CREAM Heat milk in a saucepan or double boiler until bubbles appear around the edge. To scald is to heat to just under the boiling point. A little steam will rise from the milk just before it boils. Take from heat immediately.

HOW TO MELT CHOCOLATE Place square of chocolate in a saucepan over boiling water, or in a double boiler over boiling water. Stir occasionally and when the chocolate is melted, take it from the heat and beat it until it is smooth and glossy.

HOW TO MELT JELLY AND MARMALADE Place jelly or marmalade in a saucepan over boiling water or in the top of a double boiler over boiling water. Stir occasionally and when it is melted, take it from heat and beat well. Do not cover saucepan or double boiler.

FOLLOW MANUFACTURER'S DIRECTIONS FOR USE OF ELECTRIC BEATER OR BLENDER.

HOW TO GRIND Meat, cheese, cooked vegetables, bread, dates, figs and many other products can be ground through a regular meat grinder. Adjust grinder and blades according to directions and place a plate or a sheet of waxed paper in front of the grinder.

Feed the ingredients through the grinder slowly and feed it through a second time if a finer grinding is required. When meat or cheese have been ground, run a piece of bread through the grinder to clean it. Take grinder apart and wash and dry carefully. Some grinders are equipped with a wooden block with which to press down the meat or cheese as it is fed into the grinder. If there is no block the ingredient must be pressed down with the hand.

HOW TO SERVE WINES

Serve a dry or medium dry white wine with fish.
Serve a dry white wine with poultry and white meat.
Serve red wine with red meat.
Serve red or dry white wine with cheese.
Serve a sweet white wine or dessert wine with dessert.
Serve a pink rosé wine with any poultry or meat.
Serve red wine with all game and game birds.
Serve champagne with anything or serve it with dessert.

HOW TO UNCORK A BOTTLE   Remove metal cap or wax cover, insert cork screw in center of cork and turn it until it has gone through the cork. Hold bottle firmly and draw out cork slowly. Clean inside lip of bottle with soft towel. If cork smells strongly or crumbles, the wine will probably taste of cork. Taste it before serving. There are patent cork screws available which may facilitate the drawing of the cork. Follow directions for their use. If cork should break and fall into wine, decant immediately and strain wine through a clean cloth.

HOW TO GRIND NUTS   Nuts can only be ground through a mechanical nut grinder equipped with a wooden block to press the nuts down against the perforate drum which grinds them. Repeat the grinding if necessary. If almonds are ground in a mortar the almond oil helps to form a moist almond paste which is suitable for certain baked goods and confections.

HOW TO WASH LETTUCE   Cut away outside leaves and stem of a head of lettuce and separate the leaves gently. Immerse in cold water shaking off the sand and earth that adheres to the leaves but do not break or wilt leaves. Shake off the water and place the leaves in a French wire basket and whirl or swing it to dry the leaves. If

preferred the leaves can be spread on a clean kitchen towel to dry
or they may be wrapped loosely in a clean towel. When the lettuce
is cleaned it can be stored in the refrigerator, but if it is washed an
hour or two before it is to be served it can remain in the basket or
towel until needed. The basket or towel should be kept in a cool
place.

HOW TO MEASURE AND WEIGH The first rule in measuring
is to use standard measuring cups and spoons and to always scrape
across the top with a knife or shake off any surplus so that every
measurement is *LEVEL*. Flour should be measured after sifting.
Sugars, mustard, cocoa, etc., should be measured after sifting or
sieving so that it will be free of lumps.

There are 3 teaspoons in 1 tablespoon
4 tablespoons in ¼ cup
and 16 tablespoons in 1 cup
4 cups make 1 quart
1 cup is ½ pint
2 tablespoons of butter equal 1 ounce
4 tablespoons or ¼ cup of flour equals 1 ounce

To weigh requires an accurate scale. Ingredients should be placed
on waxed paper before they are weighed for easy handling. If they
have to be weighed in a container, the empty container will have to
be weighed in order to subtract the amount from the total.

HOW TO SCRAPE BEEF Use top round of beef for scraping and
have the butcher cut it in one large slice about 1 inch thick. It is
better to use two slices than to use a thicker slice. Bring the meat
to room temperature before scraping it. Hold one end of the slice
of meat down firmly on a wooden chopping or bread board and
scrape the beef with the edge of a silver teaspoon, scraping the meat
away from you, not towards you. Do not use an old or soft silver
spoon as there is considerable pressure on the spoon. Hold the
spoon low down on the handle and face the spoon in the direction
in which you are scraping. Scrape the length of the meat in a long
stroke and turn the spoon to see how much scraped beef you are
gathering in it. It should be pure red beef without gristle or fat
and the spoon should be over half full. If you are not getting that
much beef, bear down a little harder on the spoon. Place the little

lozenge of meat from the spoon on a plate and add each spoonful to it, shaping it into a mound. Scrape the piece of beef until you are not obtaining a great deal of meat, then turn it over and scrape the other side. Continue to scrape and turn until only fat, sinew and fiber remain. Cover the meat with an inverted bowl and refrigerate it until needed, but try to scrape it just before it is needed, as it turns dark and becomes dry very quickly.

REMEMBER   You will not have to "stir briskly over gently simmering water." You will not have to "blanch" or "scald." You will not have to "sauté until golden" or "bind with an egg yolk after reducing heat to just below boiling." You will be spared the pitfalls and you will have always at hand, under a single cover, the best recipes for dishes that need no cooking. That is the reason for the NO COOKING COOKBOOK.

CHAPTER 1.

Appetizers and Hors d'Oeuvres

WHETHER you eat them in the living room with cocktails or as a first course at the table, they are the good things that most meals start with, the opening gambit, and as such they have to whet the interest and stimulate the appetite.

The appetizer or hors d'oeuvre is often neglected because of lack of time. The hostess sighs with satisfaction over the little gasp that comes from the freshly opened vacuum-packed can of nuts. She places them in a dish for her dinner guests before she returns to the pressing needs of the main course.

Dinner should start more glamorously than that. No one should be given a cocktail without a little good food to accompany it. No one should entertain a guest without leading up to the main course.

Although some of the following recipes require chopping or ricing, none of them require cooking, and only one requires heating. These are recipes for preparing new and interesting appetizers and hors d'oeuvres from the simplest combinations to others which are worthy of a gourmet dinner. None will need more than a few minutes to prepare and many can be prepared hours or days before they are needed and stored in the refrigerator. There is only one exception to the NO COOKING rule—a few recipes call for hard-cooked

23

eggs. See the HOW TO directions for How to Boil an Egg and How to Peel it after boiling.

(See also Chapter 6: CHEESE)

GUACAMOLE

2 large avocados
3 tablespoons minced onion
juice of 1 lime
½ teaspoon prepared mustard
2 tablespoons mayonnaise

2 teaspoons catsup
1 lime, thinly sliced
salt and freshly ground black
    pepper
bowl of Fritos or potato chips

Mash avocados, add next 5 ingredients, season and serve, surrounded by lime slices, as a dip for Fritos or potato chips.

ORANGES WITH AVOCADO SAUCE

3 oranges, peeled and sliced
2 avocados, peeled, seeded
    and crushed
juice of 2 limes

2 teaspoons French mustard
    (Dijon)
salt to taste

Retain any juice from slicing oranges. Whip crushed avocado with mustard and lime juice, season and pour over orange slices. Thin with orange juice if necessary.

ANTIPASTO
(The Italian First Course)

4 wedges finocchio
8 celery stalks
12 small radishes
1 cup spiced beet salad
8 slices salami

12 rolled fillets of anchovies
12 black olives
4 sardines
4 pimientos

Divide all ingredients over 4 plates, giving each serving one-quarter of the ingredients. Pass oil and vinegar separately.

MORE ELABORATE ANTIPASTO

4 hard-cooked eggs, sliced
1 cup Spiced Mushrooms (see page 32)
1 can tuna fish
½ cup pickled onions

4 slices prosciutto ham
4 celery stalks
4 slices mortadella sausage
8 radishes
8 artichoke hearts in oil

Divide all ingredients as above, giving each person one-quarter of the ingredients.

EGG DIP

2 hard-cooked eggs, chopped
2 tablespoons minced spring onion
1 smallest jar caviar
½ garlic clove
2 tablespoons minced parsley

½ teaspoon dry mustard
½ teaspoon Worcestershire sauce
mayonnaise
salt and pepper to taste

Rub a small bowl with garlic clove and discard. Stir seasonings into mayonnaise and fold in all other ingredients. Use only enough mayonnaise to hold together for a spread, add a little more for a dip. Chill and serve.

ANCHOVY SPREAD

1 can flat fillets of anchovy, drained and chopped
½ cup tiny gherkins sliced into thin rounds
2 tablespoons chopped capers

2 hard-cooked eggs, chopped
2 tablespoons chopped parsley
enough mayonnaise to hold together

Stir all ingredients together and serve with buttered pumper-nickel wedges.

SARDINE SPREAD

½ teaspoon anchovy paste
4 skinless sardines, crushed
¼ cup finely chopped onion
2 hard-cooked eggs, chopped

¼ cup creamed butter
grated rind of 1 lemon
lemon juice to taste
2 tablespoons minced chives

Mix all ingredients and serve with buttered toast rounds.

ANCHOIADE

1 can anchovy fillets
freshly ground black pepper
2 to 3 tablespoons tarragon vinegar
2 tablespoons olive oil
2 peeled, sliced and drained
    tomatoes

1 small chopped onion
2 tablespoons chopped capers
¼ cup chopped parsley
2 hard-cooked eggs, sliced and
    separated
buttered toast fingers

Drain oil from anchovies, add pepper and stir in enough vinegar to make a mild French dressing. Lay tomatoes in a serving dish, cover with rings of egg white, anchovies, onion and parsley. Pour over dressing and top with riced egg yolks. Serve cold with toast fingers.

MACEDOINE NIÇOISE

In Nice they apparently put *everything* into their Macedoines. This makes a splendid Sunday evening supper salad.

2 slices ham
2 slices chicken or turkey
2 slices salami
3 canned beets
2 stalks celery
½ green pepper
3 pieces cocktail herring
3 canned white potatoes

1 small apple, peeled and cored
½ green pepper, seeded
4 ripe pitted olives
2 hard-cooked eggs, separated
¾ cup Sauce Ravigote (see page
    174)
salt and pepper
½ head Boston lettuce, shredded

Cut first 11 ingredients into fine julienne strips, also cut egg whites into strips, combine everything with Ravigote sauce and season to taste. Serve on shredded lettuce and top with riced egg yolk.

CRAB, LOBSTER OR SHRIMP COCKTAIL

1 pound canned crab, lobster or
    shrimps
1 can grapefruit sections
¾ teaspoon Worcestershire sauce

¼ cup orange juice
¼ cup tomato catsup
6 lettuce leaves
¼ cup chopped parsley

Arrange fish and grapefruit on lettuce leaves in cocktail glasses. Mix next three ingredients and pour over fish. Dust with parsley and serve very cold.

BRUCE SHRIMP COCKTAIL

18 peeled and cooked shrimps
4 lettuce leaves
½ cup peeled chopped tomato
½ cup diced avocado
1 tablespoon chopped onion
1 tablespoon chopped green
    pepper

1 tablespoon chopped parsley
¾ cup mayonnaise
salt and pepper to taste
1 lemon, quartered

Arrange shrimps, tomato and avocado on lettuce leaves in 4 cocktail glasses or dishes. Mix onion, pepper and parsley with mayonnaise, season and pour over shrimps. Serve a lemon wedge with each glass.

THREE SEA FOODS COCKTAIL

1 can crab meat, drained
½ pound cooked shrimps
1 small container frozen lobster
    meat, thawed
juice ½ lemon
½ cup cocktail sauce
2 teaspoons minced dill

¼ cup mayonnaise
2 tablespoons drained sweet pickle
    relish
salt and pepper to taste
¼ cup each diced, peeled celery
    and cucumber

Mix all ingredients and serve on lettuce leaves.

LIVER-STUFFED MUSHROOMS

1 pound medium-sized uncooked
    mushrooms
1 3-ounce package cream cheese
2 tablespoons sour cream

¼ cup liver paté
salt and pepper to taste
1 teaspoon lemon juice
2 tablespoons chopped chives

Chop mushroom stems, mix with cheese, sour cream, paté, seasonings and lemon juice. Fill mushroom caps with the mixture and roll tops in chopped chives.

POOR MAN'S LIVER PATÉ

½ pound liver sausage
¼ cup mayonnaise
1 small onion, minced

¼ cup pecans, chopped
½ teaspoon oregano
salt and pepper

Crush the liver sausage with a fork, whip it into a smooth paste with the mayonnaise. Add all other ingredients, place in a jar and chill. Serve with crackers or buttered salty rye bread. This paté can be stored in refrigerator for several days. Serve with cocktails or as a first course.

LIVER PATÉ

2 cups, 1 pound liverwurst
¼ cup thick mayonnaise
2 tablespoons minced onion
2 tablespoons lemon juice
¼ cup shelled pistachio nuts

salt and freshly ground black
    pepper to taste
2 hard-cooked eggs, riced
3 tablespoons chopped parsley
water cress

Skin liverwurst and beat into a smooth paste, add next five ingredients, press into a round bowl and chill. Unmold onto a serving dish, rice over the hard-cooked eggs and dust with parsley. Surround with water cress and serve with crisp hot crackers or melba toast rounds.

CHICKEN LIVER PATÉ LIVORNO

2 cans chicken liver paté
3 tablespoons butter
4 minced anchovies
1 tablespoon minced parsley

1 tablespoon lemon juice
2 teaspoons onion juice
salt and pepper
¼ teaspoon thyme

Mix all ingredients. Chill and spread on toast rounds or shape into a small loaf, chill and serve slices with olives, sardines and celery as an antipasto.

RED CAVIAR WITH ONION

1 4-ounce jar red caviar
1 small onion, chopped
3 tablespoons chopped chives

2 tablespoons parsley, chopped
1 hard-cooked egg, riced

Mix all ingredients, place in a serving dish and chill. Serve with thin buttered pumpernickel or crackers.

CRAB MEAT AND CUCUMBER

1 can crab meat, drained and
  picked
3 tablespoons sweet pickle relish,
  drained
2 tablespoons mayonnaise

1 tablespoon chili sauce
2 tablespoons parsley, chopped
½ unpeeled cucumber, chopped
  fine and drained
½ teaspoon salt or to taste

Mix all ingredients. Serve chilled with thin buttered bread or crackers.

SHRIMP BUTTER

¼ pound cooked shrimps
¼ pound soft salt butter

Blend, grind or pound shrimps to a paste, mix with butter, salt to taste and chill.

LOBSTER BUTTER

Substitute lobster for shrimps, using lobster coral instead of part of the lobster meat, if it is available.

ALMOND BUTTER AND CHEESE

¼ pound butter
¼ cup blanched almonds, chopped
    fine or ground
juice and grated rind of ½ orange
salt to taste

½ pound sliced Swiss or Emmental
    cheese
thin sliced pumpernickel or rye
    bread

Cream butter, add almonds, orange juice, rind and salt. Spread on bread and serve with sliced cheese.

MELON COCKTAIL

2 cantaloupes or 2 containers
    melon balls
¼ cup walnuts, chopped fine
¼ cup mayonnaise

2 tablespoons chutney, chopped
1 tablespoon parsley, chopped
salt and pepper
lettuce leaves

Cut melon into balls with a small scoop, or defrost and drain frozen melon balls. Divide into cocktail glasses. Add chutney, parsley and seasoning to mayonnaise, pour over the melon balls and dust with walnuts.

TOMATO JUICE COCKTAIL

3 cups tomato juice
2 teaspoons vinegar
2 teaspoons celery salt

1½ teaspoons lemon juice
½ teaspoon Worcestershire sauce
1 dash Tabasco Sauce

Mix, chill and serve.

BLUE CHEESE POTATO CHIPS

½ cup Blue cheese
3 tablespoons soft butter
1 tablespoon sour cream
1 tablespoon sherry

1 teaspoon paprika
salt and pepper to taste
1 package crisp potato chips
¼ cup minced water cress

Mix first 6 ingredients into a soft paste. Spread carefully on potato chips, using only medium-sized chips, and dust with minced water cress.

FRUIT COCKTAIL

1½ cups orange sections
1 cup diced pineapple
½ cup heavy cream
1 tablespoon catsup

2 teaspoons lemon juice
salt and pepper to taste
lettuce leaves

Mix the fruit and arrange it on lettuce leaves in cocktail glasses. Combine all other ingredients, stir until smooth and pour over the fruit.

GRAPEFRUIT COCKTAIL

2 cups grapefruit sections
1 cup cold boiled shrimps
½ cup mayonnaise
¼ cup grapefruit juice
½ onion, chopped

2 tablespoons parsley, chopped
1 teaspoon prepared mustard
1 tablespoon apricot or peach jam, melted
salt and pepper to taste

Divide mixed grapefruit and shrimps onto lettuce leaves in 4 cocktail glasses. Combine all other ingredients, stir well and pour over the grapefruit.

RADISH SALAD CAPER

8 unpeeled large radishes, sliced thin
1 unpeeled cucumber, sliced thin
3 tablespoons oil
3 tablespoons vinegar
½ teaspoon salt, or to taste

¼ teaspoon pepper
3 tablespoons chopped capers
4 scallions sliced across
1 tablespoon chopped parsley
1 tablespoon chopped chives
Boston lettuce leaves

Bind radish and cucumber with oil, vinegar and seasonings. Arrange on lettuce leaves and dust with capers, scallions and herbs. Serve as a salad or as a first course.

SPICED MUSHROOMS

1 pound mushrooms, sliced thin
1 onion, chopped
1 clove garlic, crushed
¼ cup oil

2 tablespoons tarragon vinegar
1 teaspoon oregano
½ teaspoon rosemary
salt and pepper

Pour oil and vinegar over all other ingredients in a bowl. Stir carefully with a wooden spoon every twenty minutes until the mushrooms are dark and moist. Chill and serve with buttered rye bread.

SARDINE TOAST

1 can boneless sardines
1 tablespoon lemon juice
1 teaspoon grated lemon rind
2 tablespoons mayonnaise

1 tablespoon soft butter
salt and pepper
6 stuffed olives, cut into rings
buttered toast fingers

Mix first 6 ingredients. Mound on buttered toast fingers and decorate with sliced olives.

RED CAVIAR AND CHEESE

1 3-ounce package cream cheese
1 teaspoon minced onion
2 tablespoons sour cream

salt to taste
16 rounds whole wheat bread
1 small jar red caviar

Mix cheese with onion and cream into a smooth paste. Pipe around edge of small bread rounds, cut with smallest cookie cutter Fill center with well drained red caviar.

PUFFED ROUNDS

16 toast rounds
16 slices cucumber
16 slices onion

⅔ cup mayonnaise
⅓ cup grated Parmesan cheese
salt to taste

Cut toast rounds, cucumbers and onion to same size with cookie cutter. Lay cucumber on toast and top with onion. Mix next three ingredients and divide over tops of onions, push under broiler and heat for about 3 minutes with oven door open until cheese-mayonnaise is brown.

GARNISHED PICKS

1. ½ pound unsliced Swiss cheese
   ¼ pound sliced ham
   3 tablespoons prepared mustard

   Cube cheese, wrap in ham, spread with mustard. Secure with toothpicks.

2. 2 peeled and cored apples
   3 slices ham

   Cube apples, wrap in ham and secure with toothpicks.

3. Raw Beef (see Beefsteak Tartar I, II and III, pages 103-104)

   Roll meat into marbles, roll in finely chopped parsley or paprika and impale on picks.

4. Impale banana slices and blue cheese marbles.
5. Radish slices with Camembert balls.

6. Cucumber slices with cream cheese, dusted with chives.
7. Onion slices with yellow cheese.
8. Melon balls with chutney cheese.

HERBED ANCHOVIES

2 cans flat anchovy fillets
1 onion, minced
1 clove garlic, crushed
½ teaspoon powdered oregano
½ teaspoon powdered basil

½ teaspoon powdered dill
½ lemon, juice and grated rind
3 tablespoons minced green pepper
2 tablespoons minced pimiento

Spread anchovies on serving dish, mix all remaining ingredients with oil from the cans and pour over anchovies. Serve very cold with toast rounds or crackers.

LIVER SPREAD I

2 4½-ounce cans liver paté
2 tablespoons brandy
½ cup chopped walnuts

salt and pepper
1 tablespoon grated orange rind

Mix and chill, serve with crackers or bread rounds.

LIVER SPREAD II

2 4½-ounce cans liver paté
½ cup chopped blanched almonds
1 can chopped mushrooms

salt and pepper to taste
2 tablespoons sherry

Mix and chill, serve with crackers or bread rounds.

CHICKEN LIVER SPREAD III

2 4½-ounce cans chicken liver paté
2 teaspoons dried chervil
2 teaspoons grated lemon rind

½ cup chopped salted cashew nuts
1 tablespoon catsup
salt and pepper

Mix and chill, serve with crackers or bread rounds.

CHUTNEY APPLES

2 apples, peeled, cored and
    chopped
¼ cup Cream Salad Dressing # 1
1 teaspoon curry powder

¼ cup drained chutney, chopped
salt and pepper
3 tablespoons minced mint
buttered black bread rounds

Combine apple, cream dressing, mixed with curry powder and chutney. Use only enough dressing to bind. The mixture should be very dry. Season and mound on black bread rounds and dust with mint.

CHEESE ROLLS

1 3-ounce package cream cheese
1 tablespoon minced onion
1 teaspoon Worcestershire sauce

salt and pepper
6 slices bologna sausage

Mix first 4 ingredients until smooth, spread on skinned sausage. Roll up, secure with picks and chill.

Variations: mix grated horse radish with cheese and omit Worcestershire sauce. Roll with dried beef, ham, pepper ham or prosciutto instead of bologna.

RUSSIAN TOMATOES

4 small tomatoes
3 tablespoons caviar
2 tablespoons chopped onion
3 tablespoons softened and riced
    cream cheese

2 tablespoons sour cream
salt and pepper to taste
1 hard-cooked egg
4 lettuce leaves

Cut hole in top of peeled tomatoes, scoop out and fill with mixture of caviar, onion, cheese, cream and seasonings. Arrange on lettuce leaves and rice over the hard-cooked egg.

BEEF TARTAR BALLS

1 pound top round, scraped (See: How to Scrape Beef.)
¼ cup chopped onions
½ garlic clove, crushed
1 teaspoon salt
½ teaspoon freshly ground black pepper

1 teaspoon paprika
1 egg yolk
3 tablespoons water
¼ cup finely chopped parsley

Mix scraped beef with onion, garlic, salt, pepper and paprika. Shape into marble-sized balls. Dip balls into yolk, beaten with water, and allow to dry for a few minutes. Roll in parsley and serve on picks.

PEACH COCKTAIL

4 to 6 peeled peaches
⅓ cup mayonnaise
1 tablespoon heavy cream
2 teaspoons currant jelly, melted

½ teaspoon English mustard
lettuce leaves
salt and pepper to taste

Slice the peaches very thin, divide them onto lettuce leaves in 4 cocktail glasses. Combine all other ingredients, pour over the peaches and serve.

CHAPTER 2.   *Soups*

THE NO COOKING COOKBOOK does not simply suggest that you mix
one can of tomato soup with one can of pea soup and serve it. It
means that you can prepare all sorts of new combinations, and old
ones too, with canned and frozen soups or dissolved bouillon cubes.
Most of the recipes add canned fish, meat or vegetables. Some are
hot soups, some are cold, but none of the hot soups will take longer
than 15 minutes to prepare and the cold ones will need only the
time it requires to chill them. Many are made with chilled ingredients and can be served at once.

Some of the soups should be stirred together, others should be
combined in the blender. None of the soups are thickened with
butter and flour cooked together or with egg yolks which are so
easily inclined to curdle. A soup thickened with a puréed vegetable can contain as many as 300 calories less than a soup thickened
with roux.

There are recipes for more than 50 soups which are time saving,
money saving and slimming, a combination which is hard to find.

ICED WINE SOUP I

(in electric blender)

3 cans tomato soup, chilled
½ sliced cucumber
1 slice onion
1 egg yolk
½ clove garlic

salt, pepper, sugar and paprika to taste
3 tablespoons salad oil
⅔ cup white wine

In electric blender, blend soup, cucumber and onion until smooth, chill. Rub a bowl with garlic and discard. Combine seasonings with yolk and gradually stir in oil, drop by drop as for mayonnaise. Stir in wine and add cold soup. Correct seasoning, serve topped with chopped parsley. An ice cube may be placed in each cup or plate.

ICED WINE SOUP II

1 cup white wine
2 cups sour cream
1 can chopped beets and their juice
1 cucumber, peeled and diced
1 tablespoon chopped dill
2 tablespoons chopped chives

8 peeled cooked shrimps
3 hard-cooked eggs, riced
salt and pepper to taste
1 lemon sliced paper thin
ice cubes

Beat chilled wine, sour cream and beet juice until smooth and light. Add cucumber, herbs, shrimps, chopped beets, and riced eggs and season to taste. Pour into soup plates. Lay an ice cube with a lemon slice on top of it into each soup plate or cup and serve as cold as possible.

BOULA

2 cans green pea soup
1 can green turtle soup
3 tablespoons sherry, or to taste

½ cup cream, whipped
salt and pepper
¼ cup grated Parmesan cheese

Combine soups, heat to boiling, add sherry and season to taste. Top with salted whipped cream and dust cream with Parmesan.

CONSOMMÉ À L'ARCHIDUC

4 cups strong chicken consommé
4 5-minute eggs
½ teaspoon paprika

2 teaspoons minced tarragon
salt and pepper

Boil eggs exactly 5 minutes, crack shells, place in cold water for half a minute, peel carefully and serve in consommé heated to boiling with tarragon and seasonings, sprinkle eggs with paprika.

If you are rich, add a truffle, peeled, sliced and cut into diamonds.

CRAB-MUSHROOM BISQUE

1 can crab meat
2 cans condensed mushroom soup
1 cup cream
½ onion, minced

1 lemon, juice and grated rind
1 dash mushroom essence
2 tablespoons chopped walnuts
salt and pepper

Combine, heat to boiling and serve.

COLD ASPARAGUS SOUP

1 onion slice
3 sprigs parsley
1 jar frozen hollandaise sauce
1 cup cream
1 can cream of asparagus soup

1 can chicken consommé
salt and pepper
2 tablespoons sherry
¼ cup slivered ham

Blend onion, parsley, half the hollandaise sauce and cream with the soups into a smooth purée. Correct seasoning, add sherry to taste and chill. Serve with a topping of the remaining hollandaise sauce, beaten until smooth, and dusted with ham.

COLD PEA SOUP

2 cans pea soup
½ cup milk
½ cup sour cream
salt and pepper

¼ cup sour cream, whipped
2 tablespoons chopped mint
3 tablespoons sherry

Combine first 3 ingredients, season and chill. Serve topped with salted sour cream, whipped with mint. Add sherry while serving.

CURRY SOUP

1 can cream of pea soup
1 can tomato soup
½ cup cream

2 teaspoons curry powder
¼ cup cream, whipped
½ cup croutons

Heat soups and cream to boiling, stir curry powder with a little hot soup until smooth, then stir into hot soup. Serve with whipped cream and croutons.

VEGETABLE SOUP

1 can cream of corn soup
1 can cream of tomato soup
1 can chicken gumbo soup

salt and pepper
¼ cup slivered ham

Heat to boiling, season and serve topped with ham.

CORN SOUP

2 cans corn chowder
1 can cream of onion soup
salt and pepper

2 tablespoons minced green pepper
2 tablespoons minced pimiento

Combine soups, heat to boiling, season and serve topped with green and red pepper.

GUMBO

2 cans chicken gumbo soup
1 can cream of asparagus soup

¼ cup chopped salted almonds
salt and pepper

Heat soups to boiling, season and serve topped with almonds.

CONSOMMÉ RUSSE

3 cans chicken bouillon
½ cup cream, whipped
salt

4 teaspoons caviar
1 teaspoon grated lemon rind

Heat soup to boiling, top with salted whipped cream. Garnish cream with caviar and lemon rind.

CLAM BROTH

3 cups canned clam broth
½ cup tomato juice
salt and pepper

½ cup peeled, seeded, chopped
tomato
2 tablespoons chopped parsley

½ cup cream, whipped

Heat broth and tomato juice to boiling, season to taste. Add tomato and parsley and serve topped with salted whipped cream.

CELERY SOUP

1 can cream of celery soup
1 can chicken consommé
½ cup heavy cream
½ cup finely minced celery heart

¼ cup shredded almonds
salt and pepper
3 tablespoons chopped celery leaves

Combine first 5 ingredients, season, heat to boiling and serve topped with celery leaves.

SENEGALAISE

2 cans shrimp bisque
measure 1 can cream
1 tablespoon curry powder
½ cup cream, whipped

salt and pepper
8 peeled, cooked shrimps
½ cup grated coconut

Combine soup and cream, stir curry powder with a little soup until smooth, then stir into soup. Season and chill. Serve topped with salted whipped cream, shrimps and coconut.

TOMATO ORANGE SOUP

3 cans tomato soup
1 cup cream
½ cup orange juice

salt and pepper to taste
4 thin orange slices
½ cup diced avocado

Combine soup, cream and juice, season to taste and chill. Serve with one orange slice in each cup and top orange with diced avocado.

SALMON CHOWDER

1 can salmon, flaked
1 can peas
2 cans cream of celery soup
1 cup milk
1 can cream of mushroom soup

6 stuffed olives, chopped
3 tablespoons chopped onion
3 tablespoons chopped parsley
1 tablespoon capers
salt and pepper

Combine all ingredients, heat to boiling and serve. If a thinner soup is preferred, add milk to taste.

COLD TOMATO BISQUE

2 cans tomato soup
1 can crab meat
1 cup cream
½ cup milk
salt and pepper

sherry to taste
1 tablespoon sweet pickle relish
¼ cup minced cucumber
2 tablespoons minced parsley

Combine all ingredients and serve chilled.

GASPACHO I

3 tomatoes
1 cucumber
1 large onion
2 cloves garlic, crushed
½ green pepper

2 tablespoons oil
1 tablespoon vinegar or to taste
salt and pepper
ice
4 slices bread

Chop and pound first 5 ingredients into a paste. Stir in oil, little by little, add vinegar and season well. Add 2 cups chopped ice and chill. Add cold water to desired consistency. Place bread slices in soup plates and pour on gaspacho. Serve at once.

GASPACHO II

1 pound peeled tomatoes, chopped
1 cucumber, seeded and diced
2 garlic cloves, crushed
4 spring onions, chopped
6 pitted ripe olives, chopped
½ green pepper, seeded and
    chopped
¼ cup olive oil
1½ tablespoons tarragon vinegar

3 tablespoons chopped parsley
1 tablespoon chopped mint
2 teaspoons chopped marjoram
salt, pepper and cayenne
1 cup ice water
chopped ice
2 hard-cooked eggs, riced
2 thick slices brown bread, crusts
    removed and diced

Chop all ingredients together into a purée, season to taste and chill. Add ice water and chopped ice and serve topped with egg and bread. Thin with more ice water if desired.

BORSCH

(in electric blender)

1 8¼-ounce can chopped beets and
    juice
1 cup sour cream
1 cup consommé

2 tablespoons lemon juice
4 teaspoons sugar
1 teaspoon chopped dill

Blend all ingredients until smooth. Serve in chilled soup cups with 1 ice cube in each cup.

JELLIED BORSCH

3 cans jellied Borsch
½ cup sour cream, whipped
1 hard-cooked egg

1 lemon, thinly sliced
2 tablespoons minced dill
salt and pepper

Serve chilled soup topped with salted sour cream. Rice egg over cream, dust with dill and garnish with lemon wedges.

COLD AVOCADO SOUP

2 cans cream of chicken soup
1 cup cream
2 avocados

salt and pepper
1 thinly sliced lime

Peel avocados, dice meat of one and blend meat of second one with soup and cream. Season and chill. Serve in chilled cups topped with diced avocado and lime slices. Thin with milk if desired.

INDIAN AVOCADO

3 cans cream of chicken soup
1 cup half-beaten cream

2 tablespoons curry powder, or to
taste

1 cup diced avocado

Add cream beaten with curry powder. Stir until smooth, top with avocado and serve ice cold.

MADEIRA MUSHROOM SOUP

1 tablespoon chopped parsley
1 tablespoon chopped onion
2 tablespoons riced egg yolk
4 large raw mushrooms

1 can bouillon
2 cans cream of mushroom soup
3 tablespoons Madeira
salt and pepper

Combine first 3 ingredients, fill into mushrooms and float on soups heated to boiling, season and add Madeira.

BULGARIAN YOGHURT SOUP

1 3-ounce package cream cheese
1 container yoghurt
1 egg
1 can onion soup

2 cans bouillon or bouillon cubes
  and water
salt and pepper
3 tablespoons chopped parsley

Beat softened cream cheese, yoghurt and egg into a smooth paste. Bring the soups to a boil, take from fire, stir in the yoghurt mixture until smooth. Serve at once in hot soup plates, dusted with parsley.

BULGARIAN CUCUMBER SOUP

1 garlic clove, crushed
½ teaspoon salt
2 tablespoons oil
2 containers yoghurt
1 cucumber, minced

lemon juice
freshly ground black pepper
½ cup chopped walnuts
ice water
1 cup chopped ice

Stir garlic with salt, add oil and yoghurt and continue to stir until smooth. Add cucumber, lemon juice, pepper and nuts and enough ice water to make 4 cups. Pour into cold cups, dust with parsley and add chopped ice to each serving.

RUSSIAN HAM SOUP

¾ cup ground ham
1 finely chopped onion
2 egg yolks

salt and pepper to taste
¼ cup chopped parsley
3 cans strong chicken consommé

Mix ham with next 4 ingredients. Heat chicken consommé to boiling or dissolve chicken bouillon cubes in boiling water. Stir ham mixture into hot consommé and serve.

POLISH SOUP

1 can onion soup (clear)
1 cup bouillon
1 can shoestring beets and their
juice
1 tablespoon tarragon vinegar
½ teaspoon powdered cloves

1 knockwurst, skinned and thinly
sliced
salt and pepper
1 egg yolk
½ cup sour cream

Heat first 6 ingredients to boiling, season to taste and take from fire. Beat yolk into sour cream and stir into soup. Stir in enough additional heated sour cream to make four cups.

ICED PARADISE SOUP

slivered rind of 1 orange
slivered rind of 1 lemon
2 tablespoons sugar or to taste
½ cup water
1 cup orange juice
½ cup lemon juice

1 cup heavy cream
2 tablespoons kirsch
1 tablespoon Grand Marnier
1 tablespoon heavy rum
1 orange, thinly sliced
2 tablespoons minced mint

Soak slivered rinds with sugar in water for ½ hour. Add chilled juices, cream and liqueurs. Beat or blend until foamy and add sugar to taste. Serve in regular soup plates with a slice of orange dusted with mint on each serving.

PEA SOUP WITH TOMATO

2 small peeled tomatoes
2 cans cream of green pea soup
1 cup bouillon
1 cup cream
½ cup sherry
2 dashes green vegetable coloring

1 tablespoon minced onion
salt and pepper to taste
1 can tiny Norwegian shrimps
2 tablespoons mayonnaise
1 teaspoon lemon juice
1 tablespoon chopped dill

Cut tomatoes in half crosswise. Scoop out enough meat to form a cup and turn upside down on a paper towel to drain. Blend or beat soups with cream, sherry, green color, onion and seasonings. Bind drained shrimps with mayonnaise mixed with lemon juice and fill into tomato halves, dust with dill and place 1 tomato in each plate of cold green pea soup.

OXTAIL SOUP

2 cans oxtail soup
1 can bouillon
1 tablespoon minced onion
½ cup sherry

salt and pepper to taste
1 lemon cut across into paper-thin slices
2 tablespoons minced parsley

Heat soups to boiling, add onion, stir well and take from heat. Add sherry and correct seasoning. Serve with lemon slices dusted with parsley on each serving.

BOULA GRATINÉE

¾ cup cream, whipped
2 cans purée of green pea soup
2 cans green turtle consommé with meat

½ cup sherry, or to taste
salt to taste
½ cup grated Parmesan cheese

Whip cream stiff with salt to taste. Heat soups to boiling, take from fire and correct seasoning. Pour soup into 4 oven-proof cups, leaving room for thick layer of whipped cream on top. Quickly fill cups with cream, dust with cheese and run under the broiler for just a few moments to brown cheese and cream.

A little more sherry may be served with this soup at table.

MILLE FANTI

1 cup bread crumbs
½ cup grated cheese
3 eggs

1 quart boiling strong bouillon
salt and pepper
dash nutmeg

Beat crumbs and cheese into eggs until light and smooth. Place in a warm soup tureen, bring to the table and beat in boiling consommé, beating vigorously. Correct seasoning and serve immediately.

BOTVINIA

(in electric blender)

1 cucumber
1 cup minced spinach leaves
1 cup sorrel
1 cup minced beet tops
2½ cups white wine
1½ tablespoons chopped chervil
1½ tablespoons chopped tarragon

1½ tablespoons chopped parsley
1 slice finocchio, if obtainable
pinch sugar
onion slices
salt and pepper
4 slices smoked salmon
⅓ cup fresh grated horse radish

Cut half of cucumber into thin one-inch-long strips, add the rest to the greens and blend with the wine and herbs and sugar. Add onion and salt and pepper to taste and serve with a slice of salmon dusted with horse radish. Garnish with cucumber strips.

RAW SOUP

1 can slivered beets
2 cups tomato juice
¼ cup French Dressing #1

½ cup paper-thin cucumber slices
⅓ cup salted sour cream
2 tablespoons chopped chives

Blend beet juice and half the beets. Keep the rest for Chiffonade Salad. Add tomato juice and dressing and blend until smooth. Correct seasoning, chill and serve with a spoon of salted whipped sour cream with cucumber slices laid on it and dusted with chives.

CHICKEN SPINACH SOUP

(in electric blender)

2 cans chicken consommé
½ cup heavy cream
1 egg yolk
1 onion slice

½ package frozen spinach, thawed
with all moisture pressed
out
salt and pepper to taste

1 slice ham, diced

Place first 6 ingredients in blender, blend until smooth, chill. Serve topped with ham. Raw spinach leaves may be substituted for frozen.

PETROGRAD SOUP

½ pound beet tops, chopped
½ cucumber, chopped
½ can beets, chopped
½ cup tarragon vinegar
1 dill pickle, chopped
½ cup cream

1 tablespoon chopped chives
1 tablespoon chopped mint
1 teaspoon chopped tarragon
salt and pepper
chopped ice or ice cubes

Mix very finely chopped beet tops, cucumber and beets, and vinegar, and season to taste. Add pickle with its juice, and cream and chill. Just before serving add enough ice water to thin to soup consistency, add herbs, correct seasoning and serve with chopped ice or ice cubes in each soup cup.

BLENDED BOUILLON

To each 1½ cups strong bouillon add ½ cup cream and an inch of lemon peel. Blend until smooth, chill and serve.

Variations:

1. To the above quantity of soup, add 1 can chopped mushrooms and 3 sprigs of parsley before blending.
2. Add 3 onion slices and 3 sprigs parsley before blending.
3. Add 1 cup any left-over cooked vegetable before blending.

CONSOMMÉ ALBION

1 small can asparagus spears
4 cups strong chicken consommé

½ can chicken liver paté
salt and pepper

Cut asparagus spears into 1-inch lengths, discard any tough pieces. Heat to boiling in consommé, season to taste, rice chicken liver paté over soup just before serving.

CONSOMMÉ BONAL

3 cups strong chicken consommé
1 can tomato soup
2 hard-cooked eggs
1 tablespoon minced parsley
2 tablespoons soft salt butter, or to
    taste

salt and pepper
2 inside stalks celery, cut into fine
    julienne

Combine soups and chill. Rice egg yolks, add enough butter to bind into a smooth paste. Form into small balls, roll in parsley and chill. Season soup, add slivered egg whites and celery and drop in yolk balls just before serving.

JELLIED MADRILENE

3 cans jellied madrilene
½ cup canned baby peas
¼ cup pearl onions
¼ cup diced celery

2 tablespoons minced parsley
1 lemon, sliced paper thin
salt and pepper

Combine first 4 ingredients, season to taste, and chill. Serve soup covered with thin lemon slices and dusted with parsley.

CONSOMMÉ NANA

½ jar garlic croutons
½ cup grated Parmesan cheese
½ cup slivered Swiss cheese

4 5-minute eggs
4 cups boiling strong bouillon

Arrange croutons and cheeses in a hot soup tureen or casserole. Boil eggs exactly 5 minutes, break shells, dip in cold water, peel carefully and place in tureen. Pour over boiling soup and serve at once.

CONSOMMÉ CONDÉ

1 cucumber
½ can liver paté
3 cups strong chicken consommé

6 lettuce leaves
salt and pepper
2 tablespoons parsley

Cut cucumber into 4 to 6 thick slices, hollow out one side of each slice with a melon ball cutter and fill cavity with paté, roll in parsley. Heat consommé to boiling, add cucumber cups and just before serving add lettuce, shredded hair fine.

JELLIED SOUP

2 cans jellied chicken consommé
½ peeled cucumber diced
3 tablespoons sherry
2 tablespoons minced onion

2 tablespoons minced parsley
1 1-ounce jar caviar
4 slices lemon

Chill soup to medium liquid stage. Add cucumber, sherry, onion and parsley and chill 30 minutes longer. Serve in cups garnished with caviar on a lemon slice.

CONSOMMÉ BON VIVEUR

4 cups strong chicken consommé
1 can peeled truffles
½ cup rounds cut from sliced chicken

Madeira or sherry to taste
salt or pepper

Cut rounds from thin truffle slices and combine first 3 ingredients. Heat to boiling, add wine to taste and serve hot.

CONSOMMÉ WASHINGTON

3 cups strong beef bouillon
½ can beef stew
½ can sliced carrots

Madeira wine to taste
salt and pepper

Heat first 3 ingredients to boiling. Add Madeira to taste and season well.

BOUILLON RIALTO

3 cups strong beef bouillon
1 jar spaghetti and sauce
1 peeled, seeded and chopped
    tomato
1 can peeled shrimps

1 tablespoon chopped parsley
½ teaspoon basil
½ teaspoon thyme
salt and pepper

Combine all ingredients. Heat to boiling and serve.

TARTAR SOUP

3 cups cream of chicken soup
1 jar ravioli and sauce
1 small can peas

1 small can cauliflower
salt and pepper
¼ cup chopped parsley

Heat all ingredients to boiling and serve.

VALROMEY

3 cups strong chicken consommé
¾ cup diced lobster meat
¾ cup canned wild rice

Marsala wine to taste
salt and pepper

Combine first 3 ingredients. Heat to boiling, add wine and seasoning and serve very hot.

COLD LOBSTER SOUP

2 cups cream
1 can tomato soup
1 can cream of mushroom soup
1 can lobster

1 tablespoon minced onion
1 tablespoon minced parsley
2 tablespoons sherry or to taste

Mix, chill and serve.

COLD CRAB SOUP

½ cucumber, sliced
½ cup heavy cream
2 teaspoons Worcestershire sauce
1 tablespoon prepared mustard
2 cans cream of mushroom soup

salt, pepper and paprika
1 pound crab meat, picked
2 tablespoons sherry
2 teaspoons minced dill

Blend first 5 ingredients into a smooth soup. Season and chill. Add crab meat and sherry and serve dusted with dill.

OYSTER CONSOMMÉ

3 cups boiling chicken consommé
12 small oysters
¼ cup sherry, or to taste

2 tablespoons minced parsley
salt and pepper

Place 3 oysters each into 4 hot bouillon cups. Pour over boiling consommé, add sherry, parsley and seasonings and serve.

COLD SHRIMP SOUP

1 pound peeled, cooked shrimps
1 cup cream
1 cup milk
1 small onion, sliced

½ teaspoon anchovy paste, or to taste
salt and pepper
¼ cup chopped green pepper

2 tablespoons chopped chives

Hold 8 shrimps aside for garnish, place cream in blender with 3 or 4 shrimps and a slice of onion, and blend into a smooth purée. Gradually add remaining shrimps and onion and finally add anchovy paste to taste. Add milk and increase milk, if necessary, to desired consistency. Correct seasoning and serve chilled with green pepper and chives passed separately.

CLAM CHOWDER

1 can sliced potatoes, diced
1 4-ounce can sliced mushrooms
2 cans minced clams
1 cup canned, drained tomatoes
2 cans condensed vegetable soup
¼ cup minced green pepper

¼ cup minced celery
1 pinch basil
1 pinch thyme
1 pinch sage
salt and pepper to taste

Heat all ingredients to boiling, being sure potatoes are heated thoroughly. Serve with hard crackers.

HOT SALMON CHOWDER

1 can sliced carrots
1 onion, sliced and divided into
    rings
2 8-ounce cans salmon, flaked
1 large can evaporated milk
½ cup heavy cream
2 cans cream of mushroom soup

¼ cup chopped green pepper
¼ cup chopped celery
½ clove crushed garlic
1 pinch thyme
2 tablespoons minced parsley
salt and pepper to taste

Heat all ingredients to boiling. Serve with hard crackers or hot garlic bread.

CHAPTER 3.   *Fish*

THAT special talent for fish cookery, which even the most experienced cooks often seem to lack, is not necessary here. The NO COOKING fish recipes are based only on raw clams and oysters or on easily obtainable canned and frozen fish and shell fish.

The most important thing to be said about fish and sea food, and it has been said often before, is the importance of making *fish* more important. Too many people know too little about fish. They go to sea food restaurants, they order shrimps and lobsters when they go out to a restaurant, but only a small percentage of the cooking cooks prepare it at home. It is to be hoped that the NO COOKING cooks will gain confidence from these recipes and include more fish on their menus.

The fish recipes can be used for first courses, main courses, luncheons, and buffets. Most of them can be prepared in advance and stored in the refrigerator.

Fish chowders are included in this chapter as they are better adapted to being a main fish course than a first-course soup.

ITALIAN SHRIMP CASSEROLE

1 can cream of pea soup
1 tablespoon minced onion
1 tablespoon sherry
2 cups drained canned corn
1 jar pimiento, drained and diced

1 pound peeled, cooked shrimps
salt, pepper
1 hard-cooked egg
2 tablespoons chopped parsley

Combine first 6 ingredients in a buttered casserole and season to taste. Heat to boiling in a moderately hot 375° F oven and serve with egg riced over the top and sprinkled with parsley.

SALMON CASSEROLE

1 can salmon, flaked
1 can sliced mushrooms, drained
1 can baby lima beans, drained

1 can cream of mushroom soup
salt and pepper
2 tablespoons chopped parsley

Combine first 4 ingredients in a buttered shallow casserole and season to taste. Heat to boiling in a moderately hot 375° F oven and serve sprinkled with parsley.

SEA FOOD CASSEROLE

1 can shrimp bisque
1 can crab meat, picked and flaked
1 can smallest green peas, drained

1 pound peeled, cooked shrimps
salt, pepper
1 small avocado peeled and diced

Combine first 4 ingredients in a buttered casserole and season to taste. Heat to boiling in a moderately hot 375° F oven and serve topped with diced avocado.

LOBSTER NEWBURG

1½ pounds frozen lobster meat
1 can button mushrooms
1 can wild rice

2 tablespoons sherry, or to taste
1 can Newburg Sauce
salt, pepper

Arrange lobster and mushrooms on the rice in a buttered

casserole. Add sherry to Newburg Sauce, season and pour over the ingredients in the casserole. Cover and heat to boiling in a moderately hot 375° F oven. Serve at once.

SHRIMP CARDINAL

1 can lobster bisque	2 pounds peeled, cooked shrimps
½ cup heavy cream	¼ cup chopped ripe olives
1 egg yolk	2 tablespoons chopped chives or
salt, pepper	parsley

Beat first three ingredients together until they are smooth. Season to taste and pour over shrimps. Chill and serve sprinkled with olives and chives or parsley.

LOBSTER ALEXANDRA

2 pounds cold cooked lobster meat	2 peeled tomatoes, drained and
1 cup sauce Alexandra	chopped
1 small head Boston lettuce	1 lemon, quartered
2 hard-cooked eggs	parsley rosettes

Cut lobster meat into large chunks, leaving claws whole. Mix with sauce Alexandra (see page 176) and arrange on shredded lettuce. Rice egg white over the lobster and rice egg yolk over the white in a cross, leaving 4 wedges of egg white. Arrange tomato slices around the lobster and serve as a main dish garnished with lemon wedges and parsley.

SHRIMP PRIMAVERA

1 pound peeled, cooked shrimps	¼ clove garlic, crushed
½ cup mayonnaise	1 bunch spring onions or scallions
2 tablespoons tarragon vinegar	salt and pepper to taste
1 tablespoon prepared mustard	

Mix mayonnaise, vinegar, mustard and garlic. Mince half the spring onions very fine and stir them into the sauce, season to taste and pour over cold cooked shrimps. Cut remaining spring onions into thin rounds and chop the tender part of the green tops. Serve shrimps with the sauce and sprinkle with the remaining onions.

PARADISE SHRIMP

24 peeled and cooked shrimps
2 tablespoons tarragon vinegar
2 tart red apples, cored
1 celery heart with root and yellow leaves
¼ cup French Dressing # 1

¼ cup thick mayonnaise
1 lemon, juice and grated rind
1 tablespoon minced chives
½ cucumber, sliced paper thin
1 small head Boston lettuce
2 tablespoons chopped parsley

Sprinkle cooked shrimps with vinegar and chill for 1 hour stirring several times. Chop apples and celery and mix with dressing. Stir mayonnaise with lemon and chives and pour over shrimps. Line salad bowl with lettuce leaves, mound apple salad in center and cover completely with cucumber slices. Surround with a border of shrimps dusted with parsley.

LOBSTER MAYORA

2 avocados, cut in half lengthwise, stone removed
1 pound lobster meat
1 tomato, peeled, seeded and chopped
½ cup mayonnaise

½ cup whipped cream
1 tablespoon tomato paste
1 lime, juice and grated rind
salt and pepper to taste
½ bunch cleaned water cress
4 lettuce leaves

Arrange avocados on lettuce leaves. Combine lobster, tomato and bind with a sauce made of next 5 ingredients. Fill into avocados. Chop water cress leaves. Bury lobster-filled avocados under generous topping of water cress. Chill and serve.

TOMATO TONATO

2 peeled tomatoes, cut in half
    crosswise
1 can tuna fish, flaked
¼ cup chopped raw cauliflower
½ onion, chopped
2 tablespoons chopped parsley

½ cup French Dressing # 1
1 can kidney beans, drained
1 white onion, sliced thin and
    divided into rings
salt and pepper

Scoop some pulp out of tomato halves. Fill with tuna fish mixed with cauliflower, onion, parsley and French dressing. Add remaining French dressing to kidney beans and arrange a border of beans around tomatoes. Top beans with onion rings and serve very cold.

MIXED SEA FOOD

½ cup chopped radishes
¼ cup chopped onion
¼ cup chopped celery
¼ cup chopped cucumber
½ cup mayonnaise
1 can crab meat
1 pound canned or cooked shrimps

1 ½-pound can lobster meat
¼ cup chopped parsley
¾ cup lemon mayonnaise
3 tablespoons French dressing
1 tablespoon sherry
salt and pepper

Combine first 5 ingredients. Arrange in center of a serving platter. Surround with sea food, dusted with parsley. Combine next 4 ingredients and pass separately as sauce for the sea food.

SHRIMP PATÉ

1 pound peeled, cooked shrimps,
    chopped
1 can rolled fillets of anchovy,
    drained

5 tablespoons butter
¼ cup white wine
freshly ground black pepper
1 teaspoon grated lemon rind

Blend or mash shrimps and anchovies into a smooth paste with butter and wine. Season to taste and chill before serving.

COLD SALMON WITH GREEN SAUCE

2 cans salmon, flaked
4 spring onions, chopped
4 stuffed olives, chopped
2 hard-cooked eggs, sliced
½ cucumber, seeded and chopped
2 radishes, chopped
salt and pepper to taste
½ dill pickle, chopped
1 cup mayonnaise

2 teaspoons minced parsley
2 teaspoons minced dill
4 spinach leaves, ground or
    blended to a paste
2 tablespoons sour cream
½ head Boston lettuce
1 lemon, quartered
parsley sprigs for garnish

Combine first 8 ingredients. Beat mayonnaise with next 4 ingredients, season to taste and pour over salmon. Arrange in lettuce-lined bowl, garnish with lemon quarters and parsley. Serve very cold.

COLD TUNA

½ cup mayonnaise
½ teaspoon minced onion
1 tablespoon minced parsley
½ teaspoon dry mustard
1 teaspoon capers

1 can tuna fish, flaked
¼ cup finely chopped celery
1 hard-cooked egg white, chopped
1 hard-cooked egg yolk, riced

Combine mayonnaise with next 4 ingredients. Combine tuna and celery and bind with the mayonnaise. Top with hard cooked egg and serve.

COLD SALMON

1 can salmon, flaked
½ cup chopped peeled cucumber
½ cup mayonnaise
1 tablespoon capers

1 teaspoon chopped fresh or dried
    dill
1 squeeze lemon juice
½ teaspoon salt or to taste

Mix all ingredients and serve.

BLUE POINTS ON THE HALF SHELL
for 6

36 blue point oysters
crushed ice
2 cups cocktail sauce

6 sprigs parsley
2 lemons, quartered
oyster crackers

Open oysters and keep in the deep half of the shell. Place six oysters each on 6 soup plates of crushed ice. Center with 6 small containers of cocktail sauce. Garnish each plate with lemon wedges and parsley and serve with crackers.

Cocktail Sauce:

1 cup tomato catsup
⅓ cup chili sauce
3 tablespoons grated horse radish
3 tablespoons minced onion
3 tablespoons minced green pepper
1 tablespoon vinegar

½ tablespoon A-1 Sauce
1 teaspoon Worcestershire sauce
1 teaspoon salt
½ teaspoon sugar
1 dash Tabasco Sauce

Mix and serve.

LOBSTER CASSEROLE

3 7-ounce cans frozen lobster, cubed
½ cup cream
¼ cup sherry
1 7-ounce can tomatoes

¼ cup black olives, chopped
1 can wild rice
salt and pepper to taste

Combine all ingredients in a buttered casserole. Heat in a 375° F oven until bubbling.

CRAB MEAT CASSEROLE

2 12-ounce packages frozen crab
    meat, picked
1 can green peas
1 can cream of mushroom soup

½ cup cream
½ cup dry bread crumbs
salt and pepper to taste

Combine all ingredients in a buttered casserole. Heat in a 375° F oven until bubbling.

LOBSTER IN HALF MOURNING

2 large containers frozen lobster,
    diced
6 tablespoons sherry
½ cup cream, whipped
salt and pepper

3 tablespoons chili sauce
3 tablespoons mayonnaise
¼ cup finely chopped black olives
2 tablespoons finely chopped
    parsley

Marinate well-drained lobster in sherry for an hour, turning it frequently. Whip cream, season well, add chili sauce and mayonnaise. Pour sauce over lobster, top with olives and parsley and serve.

KEDGEREE SALAD

2 teaspoons curry powder, or to
    taste
¾ cup mayonnaise
¼ cup minced chutney
salt and pepper

2 cups cold cooked rice
1 cup flaked crab meat
1 chopped onion
2 hard-cooked eggs, riced

Stir curry powder into mayonnaise, add chutney and season to taste. Pour sauce over rice, crab meat and onion and stir well. Arrange salad in a bowl and top with riced eggs.

CITRUS LOBSTER

2 chilled grapefruit
4 oranges, cut into sections, free of
    membranes, pits and rind

1 pound cooked lobster meat, diced
lettuce leaves

Cut grapefruit in half, loosen sections and take out with a spoon in perfect pieces if possible. Scrape out shells and discard membranes and core. Retain grapefruit juice. Mix grapefruit sections, orange sections and lobster and refill shells. Place on lettuce leaves and pour over special dressing.

½ cup grapefruit juice
¼ cup salad oil
2 tablespoons vinegar
½ teaspoon salt
1 teaspoon sugar

½ teaspoon paprika
½ teaspoon mustard
¼ cup chili sauce
¼ cup mayonnaise

Mix or blend all ingredients and pour over filled grapefruit halves.

OYSTERS WITH ANCHOVY CHEESE

24 oysters on the half shell
½ 8-ounce package cream cheese
2 tablespoons anchovy paste, or to
    taste

3 tablespoons minced parsley
1½ cups catsup

Prepare oysters as directed for oysters on the half shell. Rice a little anchovy cheese over each, top with parsley and serve with catsup.

OYSTERS IN MUSHROOMS

12 large mushrooms
1 cup French dressing
salt and pepper

12 bearded oysters
½ cup catsup
2 tablespoons chopped chives

Marinate stemmed mushroom caps in French dressing, turning them frequently until they are dark. Drain and season. Fill each cap with an oyster dipped in catsup. Dust with chives and serve.

OYSTERS VIRGINIA

24 oysters on the half shell
1 cup catsup
1 lemon, quartered

½ cup herb butter
salt and pepper to taste
4 slices ham, minced

Prepare oysters as for oysters on the half shell with catsup and lemon wedges. Place a tiny scoop of cold herb butter on each oyster, season and top with minced ham.

OYSTER MUSHROOM CHOWDER

1 can cream of oyster soup	salt and pepper
2 cans cream of mushroom soup	24 oysters
1 tablespoon grated onion	2 tablespoons butter
½ cup cream	2 teaspoons paprika

Heat first 4 ingredients to boiling, season, add oysters and butter and dust with paprika.

OYSTER CHOWDER

1 can sliced potatoes, diced	1 small onion, minced
1 can corn	24 oysters
2 cups milk	1 tablespoon butter
salt and pepper to taste	3 tablespoons minced parsley

Heat first 5 ingredients to boiling, add oysters, butter and parsley and serve at once.

OYSTER-STUFFED EGGS

4 hard-cooked eggs	8 oysters
1 tablespoon grated horse radish	½ cup catsup
2 tablespoons mayonnaise	¼ cup mayonnaise
salt and pepper	hickory-smoked salt

Cut eggs in half lengthwise, rice yolks, mix with horse radish and mayonnaise and season to taste. Place a small oyster in each egg half, top with yolk mixture and serve with a mixture of catsup and mayonnaise and a little hickory-smoked salt on the side.

CLAMS ON THE HALF SHELL

24 clams
1 lemon, quartered
½ cup grated horse radish

Tabasco Sauce
Worcestershire sauce
crushed ice

Open clams, serve on half the shell, arrange 6 clams each on 4 plates of crushed ice. Place a small glass of cocktail sauce in the center, garnish with lemon wedges and pass remaining ingredients on the side.

Cocktail Sauce:

½ cup catsup
2 tablespoons lemon juice
¼ teaspoon Tabasco Sauce
1 tablespoon vinegar
salt and pepper to taste

RED AND GREEN SHRIMPS

1 pound peeled, cooked shrimps
2 tomatoes, peeled and diced
6 chopped stuffed olives
6 chopped radishes
½ cup chopped celery
½ cucumber, diced

½ green pepper, diced
½ bunch water cress, stems
removed and chopped
1 cup French dressing
1 head Boston lettuce

Mix all ingredients, bind with dressing and arrange in lettuce-lined salad bowl.

LOBSTER ERICA

4 1½-pound boiled lobsters
1 cup mayonnaise
2 tablespoons minced capers
8 lettuce leaves
2 peeled tomatoes, halved

1 can mixed vegetables
½ cup lemon mayonnaise
4 hard-cooked eggs
anchovy paste to taste

Cut lobsters in half, clean and fill cavity with mayonnaise mixed with green lobster fat, any red lobster coral available and chopped capers. Set lobster halves on lettuce leaves on 4 plates and accompany each serving with ½ tomato filled with vegetables bound with lemon mayonnaise and 1 hard-cooked egg, yolk removed and beaten with anchovy paste and returned to egg whites.

SHRIMP SALAD I

1 pound peeled, cooked shrimps
1 cucumber, peeled and diced
¾ cup chopped water cress
3 tablespoons grated horse radish

¾ cup mayonnaise
salt and pepper to taste
½ head Boston lettuce
2 tomatoes, peeled and sliced

Line a salad bowl with Boston lettuce leaves, mix first four ingredients with mayonnaise, season and serve surrounded by tomato slices.

SHRIMP SALAD II

1 pound peeled, cooked shrimps
1 cup celery cut into julienne strips
1 cup diced melon or melon balls
¼ cup French dressing
½ teaspoon minced or dried
    tarragon

½ teaspoon minced or dried
    chervil
½ cup mayonnaise
¼ cup chili sauce
salt and pepper

Combine first 6 ingredients and chill. Just before serving, drain and bind with mayonnaise and chili sauce. Season to taste and serve.

SHRIMPS PASCAL

1 cup chopped cooked shrimps
1 diced sour apple
½ cup chopped celery
¾ cup diced boiled potatoes,
    canned

¼ cup chopped onion
¾ cup mayonnaise
salt and pepper
3 sliced, peeled tomatoes
1 tablespoon snipped dill

Combine first 5 ingredients with mayonnaise, season to taste, arrange on tomato slices and dust with dill.

PALM SHRIMP

1 can hearts of palm
1 pound peeled, cooked shrimps
¼ cup mayonnaise
¼ cup French dressing
2 tablespoons catsup

1 small onion, chopped
1 hard-cooked egg, riced
2 tablespoons capers, chopped
2 tablespoons chopped parsley

Cut hearts of palm into inch-long rounds, add shrimps and bind with mayonnaise mixed with dressing, catsup and onion. Arrange on a serving dish, cover with egg, capers and parsley. Serve very cold as a luncheon dish.   .

JAPANESE SHRIMP SALAD

1 cup peeled, cooked shrimps
¼ cup tarragon vinegar
½ cup mayonnaise
¼ cup sour cream
1 can button mushrooms

¾ cup diced cold chicken meat
¾ cup chopped celery
½ cup canned green peas
salt and pepper to taste
2 tablespoons chopped mint

Marinate shrimps in vinegar for 1 hour, stirring frequently. Whip mayonnaise with sour cream and season to taste. Combine next four ingredients with shrimps and vinegar, bind with the mayonnaise and serve dusted with mint.

LOBSTER IN CHAMPAGNE

1½ pounds cooked lobster meat,
    diced
3 hard-cooked eggs, separated
3 tablespoons butter

salt, pepper and cayenne
1 pinch of mace
1 to 2 splits champagne
1 lemon, quartered

Arrange lobster in pan. Pound egg yolks with butter and seasonings, add to lobster, cover with champagne and heat just to boiling. Serve with lemon and riced egg whites.

CRAB MEAT

1 pound canned or frozen crab
    meat, thawed and drained
¼ cup chili sauce
1 tablespoon sherry
¼ cup mayonnaise

salt and pepper to taste
½ lemon, juice and grated rind
1 pinch dry mustard
lettuce leaves

Divide crab meat into 4 portions onto lettuce leaves. Mix all other ingredients, pour over crab meat and serve very cold.

LITTLE NECK CLAMS

36 little necks
6 lemon wedges

crushed ice
6 parsley sprigs

Arrange 6 clams each on six soup plates of crushed ice, garnish with lemon wedges and parsley and serve Spring Onion Sauce separately.

SPRING ONION SAUCE

1 bunch scallions or spring onions
1 shallot, minced

1 teaspoon freshly crushed pepper
1 cup vinegar

Slice peeled scallions across thinly. Mix with minced shallot, vinegar and pepper and pass with clams.

REBUMBO

1 package frozen crab meat, thawed
1 package frozen lobster, thawed
2 tablespoons mayonnaise
2 tablespoons catsup
2 tablespoons sherry

juice and grated rind of ½ lemon
2 teaspoons horse radish, drained
1 pinch English mustard powder
1 cup green seedless grapes

Pick crab meat and lobster to remove any membranes or shells. Remove stems from grapes. Mix all ingredients, chill and serve.

ICED SHRIMP CURRY

1 pound peeled, cooked shrimps
2 teaspoons curry powder
2 teaspoons soft butter
¾ cup mayonnaise
½ cup minced onion

½ cup minced green pepper
¼ cup chopped pimiento
2 hard-cooked eggs, riced
¼ cup minced parsley

Stir curry into soft butter until smooth, gradually whip into mayonnaise; for a really hot curry, add more curry and butter to taste. Bind shrimps with mayonnaise and mound in center of serving platter, dust all other ingredients over the top. Mix all ingredients only when serving.

LOBSTER CREAM

2 cups cold cooked lobster meat
½ teaspoon dry mustard
3 tablespoons clam juice
1¼ cups mayonnaise
⅓ cup tomato sauce
1 tablespoon sherry

1 teaspoon chopped mint
salt and pepper
½ cup sour cream
¼ each teaspoon fresh or dry
    minced parsley, chervil,
    chives and mint

Stir mustard into a little clam juice until smooth. Mix with mayonnaise and next 3 ingredients, season and add to lobster. Divide into chilled cocktail glasses and top with sour cream whipped with herbs.

SKEWERED SHRIMPS

24 shrimps
1 lemon, quartered
1½ cups mayonnaise
2 tablespoons bouillon
2 tablespoons mild French mustard
juice and grated rind of ½ lemon

½ teaspoon dry mustard
½ teaspoon chopped or dry
    rosemary
1 dash Maggi
parsley for garnish

Impale 6 shrimps each on 4 skewers and end with a lemon wedge. Lay skewers on chopped ice, garnish with parsley and serve with a sauce made of all remaining ingredients.

COLD MARINATED SEA FOOD

1 cup olive oil
¾ cup tarragon vinegar
¼ cup clam juice
3 tablespoons white wine
1 onion, finely diced

1 tablespoon minced chives
1 tablespoon minced shallots
½ teaspoon salt, or to taste
¼ teaspoon pepper

1 pound cooked lobster meat
1 pound cooked crab meat
12 peeled, cooked shrimps
1 peeled tomato, sliced
½ cup chopped celery

½ cup cherry tomatoes
6 chopped radishes
6 to 8 whole small radishes
3 scallions, cut across into rounds
iceberg lettuce, shredded

Mix first 9 ingredients into a smooth dressing. Divide sea food, sliced tomato, and all remaining ingredients, except whole radishes, onto shredded lettuce on large plates and pour dressing over. Top with whole radishes and serve very cold. This can also be served as a single dish, packed in ice to which guests help themselves. An excellent buffet or luncheon dish.

NORWEGIAN SALMON

1 can lobster, diced
1 jar caviar
½ teaspoon tarragon
1 tablespoon mustard
1 cup mayonnaise
salt and pepper
3 small cucumbers, peeled

3 slices smoked salmon
6 very small tomatoes, peeled and
 hollowed out
½ small head iceberg lettuce,
 shredded
1 can salmon, flaked
1 lemon, sliced

Combine diced lobster with next 4 ingredients, season to taste and chill. Cut cucumbers in half the long way and scoop out seeds, making 6 little "boats." Mince or grind smoked salmon, fill into boats and grind pepper over top. Fill lobster sauce into tomatoes and arrange around a large serving platter covered with shredded lettuce. Set the cucumber boats between the tomatoes and center the platter with the flaked salmon. Garnish with lemon slices and serve.

SHRIMPS ON GRAPEFRUIT

2 large grapefruit
1 pound peeled, cooked shrimps
2 tablespoons minced onion
1 cup thick mayonnaise
2 to 3 tablespoons grapefruit juice

2 tablespoons apricot or peach jam
1 teaspoon lemon juice
grated rind of 1 lemon
2 tablespoons minced parsley
salt and pepper to taste

Cut grapefruit in half and cut out center with a sharp knife leaving a 2-inch hollow. Loosen sections and retain all juice. Fill centers with shrimps, pour over them a sauce made of all remaining ingredients and serve very cold.

CLAMS ON GRAPEFRUIT

2 large grapefruit
1 container or 24 fresh clams
½ cup chili sauce
Tabasco Sauce

salt and freshly ground black
   pepper
1 tablespoon chopped spring onion
3 tablespoons grated horse radish

Cut grapefruit as for Shrimps on Grapefruit and fill centers with drained clams. Combine chili sauce with Tabasco and seasonings and pour over clams. Top with onion and horse radish and serve very cold.

LOBSTER VIVIDA

1 envelope gelatine
3 tablespoons lemon juice
½ cup boiling water
1½ cups mayonnaise
2 cans mixed vegetables, drained
2 tablespoons minced parsley
salt and pepper to taste

1 pound container lobster meat
2 tablespoons tarragon vinegar
2 tablespoons olive oil
2 hard-cooked eggs, sliced
1 1-ounce jar caviar
½ bunch water cress

Empty gelatine into a cup, add lemon juice and set aside to soften for 10 minutes. Pour boiling water over gelatine and stir until it dissolves, cool and combine with mayonnaise. Add mixed vegetables, parsley and season, pour into a round bowl or mold and chill until set, about 1 hour. Leave lobster claws whole, cut remaining meat into chunks and season to taste. Sprinkle with vinegar and oil and chill. Unmold vegetable salad onto center of serving platter. Cover with lobster meat and garnish with egg slices, centered with little mounds of caviar. Surround with water cress and pass a little mayonnaise separately.

COLD SALMON BELLE VUE

1 can mixed vegetables, drained
½ cup thick mayonnaise
1 can salmon, flaked
1½ cups Sauce Rémoulade
3 hard-cooked eggs, halved

6 cooked, peeled shrimps
6 medium mushrooms
6 lemon wedges
¼ cup minced parsley

Mix mayonnaise with vegetables and arrange 6 small mounds around a serving platter. Center with salmon, bound lightly with Rémoulade Sauce, and place remaining sauce into a glass bowl to pass separately. Arrange egg halves between vegetable mounds and place a shrimp on each, intersperse with lemon wedges and 6 raw mushrooms cleaned and filled with chopped parsley, bound with a little of the Rémoulade Sauce.

OYSTERS

24 small oysters on the half shell
1 lemon, quartered

⅓ cup chopped spring onion
3 ounces fresh caviar

Arrange oyster on the half shell on shaved ice as usual with lemon. Pass spring onions and caviar instead of cocktail sauce and horse radish.

CRAB MEAT MOUSSELINE

2 cups picked crab meat
1 cup mayonnaise
½ teaspoon paprika, or to taste
salt and pepper
½ teaspoon grated lemon rind

1 teaspoon lemon juice
2 egg whites, beaten stiff
2 tablespoons chopped parsley and
    paprika for garnish

Chill crab meat, mix mayonnaise with next 4 ingredients, fold in egg whites and crab meat. Dust with a little paprika and top with parsley.

LOBSTER MOUSSE

1 envelope gelatine
¼ cup white wine or water
½ cup boiling water
1 egg white, beaten stiff
½ cup cream, whipped

salt to taste
3 cups frozen or canned minced
    lobster meat
2 cups fruit or cucumber salad
1 cup lemon mayonnaise

Empty gelatine into cup, add wine or water, soften for 10 minutes, add boiling water and stir until gelatine is dissolved, cool. Fold egg white into whipped cream, add seasoned lobster and cooled gelatine. Pour into a rinsed mold and set in coldest part of refrigerator for at least 2 hours. Unmold on a chilled platter, garnish with fruit or cucumber salad and pass mayonnaise separately.

COLD COQUILLES

1 pound canned or cooked scallops
½ package frozen or 1 8-ounce can
    small cooked shrimps
1 can chopped mushrooms
3 tablespoons chopped parsley

3 tablespoons chopped onion
salt and pepper to taste
¾ cup lemon mayonnaise
1 hard-cooked egg
parsley sprigs for garnish

Chop scallops if they are large, combine with next 4 ingredients, season and divide into 6 scallop shells. Mask with mayonnaise, rice hard-cooked egg over the top and garnish with parsley. (Crab meat may be substituted for the scallops.)

CHAPTER 4.   *Eggs*

THERE has to be an exception to every rule and in this case it appears among the eggs. The NO COOKING cook will have to cook after all. If she doesn't know how to already, she is going to have to learn to hard-cook an egg and to half-cook an egg, which the French call an Egg Mollet, and substitute so successfully for our poached eggs.

This chapter also requires the breaking and separating of an egg and the beating stiff of an egg white (see the cooking verbs, HOW TO BREAK AN EGG, etc., for all directions). As far as beating an egg white to the desired stiffness is concerned, beat it until you could hold the bowl over your head without disaster, or until you can tilt the bowl of stiff egg white without its sliding or moving at all.

The egg recipes are for first courses, luncheon dishes, Lent and all other occasions when a new kind of an egg is welcome. The stuffed eggs can be prepared for a cocktail party, a buffet or a first course. The recipes for eggs mollet can be made with warm or cold eggs, depending on the season.

74

BARCELONA EGGS

4 5-minute eggs
2 peeled tomatoes
1 jar frozen Béarnaise sauce

2 tablespoons minced parsley or
    chives
4 lettuce leaves

4 gherkins, cut into fans

Crack egg shells carefully, lay eggs in cold water. Cut tomatoes in half, across, scoop out pulp and drain well. Peel eggs carefully, lay into tomato cup and cover with well-whipped Béarnaise
sauce. Top with parsley and arrange tomatoes on lettuce leaves.
Garnish each serving with a gherkin fan.

HERBED SLICED EGGS

4 hot hard-cooked eggs, sliced
2 tablespoons parsley, finely
    chopped
2 teaspoons chervil, finely chopped
2 shallots, finely chopped

2 teaspoons chives, finely chopped
4 lettuce leaves
salt and freshly ground pepper
½ cup mayonnaise
juice of ½ lemon

Slice hard-cooked eggs onto lettuce leaves. Cover with herbs
and shallots and serve hot with mayonnaise to which lemon juice
has been added.

RUSSIAN EGGS

3 hard-cooked eggs
6 tablespoons caviar

grated rind of ½ lemon
3 tablespoons sour cream

Cut eggs in half, take out yolks and fill whites with caviar.
Add lemon rind to sour cream and divide over 6 egg halves. Rice
yolks over the sour cream and serve.

EGGS FILBERT

6 hot hard-cooked eggs
2 tablespoons heavy cream
½ teaspoon curry powder or to
    taste

salt and pepper
¼ cup chopped hazel nuts (or
    filberts)

Halve hot eggs, rice yolks, pound with cream, curry powder and seasonings. Refill eggs, sprinkle with nuts and serve at once.

EGGS BONNE FEMME

6 hard-cooked eggs
¼ cup mayonnaise
1 tablespoon whipped cream
1 teaspoon chopped fresh or dried
    tarragon

salt and pepper
½ bunch water cress
¾ cup sliced beets
¼ cup French dressing

Cut eggs in half lengthwise, rice yolks and mix with mayonnaise, cream, tarragon and seasonings. Fill yolk mixture into whites, arrange on water cress and garnish with beet slices marinated in French dressing.

ALLIGATOR EGGS

2 small avocados
4 5-minute eggs
¼ cup French dressing

¼ cup mayonnaise
1 minced pimiento
salt and pepper

Cut avocados across, take out stones and cut slice from bottom to stand avocados upright. Pour French dressing into avocados and marinate for 20 minutes. In the meantime, boil eggs just 5 minutes, break shells carefully and lay in cold water. As soon as eggs are cold, carefully draw off shells. Set 1 egg in each avocado half and pour over seasoned mayonnaise mixed with pimiento.

CURRIED EGGS I

1 cup chopped ham
¾ cup mayonnaise
2 teaspoons curry powder

4 5-minute eggs
2 tablespoons chopped parsley

Stir curry powder to a smooth paste with a little mayonnaise, then stir in rest of mayonnaise, mix with ham, top with cold eggs and dust with parsley.

CURRIED EGGS II

2 cups cold boiled rice
salt and pepper
¼ cup heavy cream
½ cup chutney

4 5-minute eggs
½ cup curry mayonnaise
½ cup chopped walnuts

Season rice well and bind with cream; increase cream if necessary. Top with chutney and eggs, pour mayonnaise over and sprinkle with nuts.

COLD CURRIED EGGS

8 hard-cooked eggs, sliced
1½ cups curried mayonnaise
salt and pepper to taste
1 can small white onions, drained
¼ cup French dressing

2 cups cold boiled rice
3 tablespoons raisins
3 tablespoons slivered almonds
¾ cup chutney
1 package coconut

Cover eggs and onions with curried mayonnaise, surround with rice mixed with dressing, raisins and almonds. Dust with coconut and garnish with little mounds of chutney. Chill and serve.

COLD SWEDISH EGGS

4 5-minute boiled eggs, chilled
4 thick slices peeled tomatoes
1 cup mayonnaise
2 tablespoons grated horse radish

2 tablespoons minced chives
2 tablespoons minced pimiento
salt and freshly ground black
    pepper

Arrange peeled eggs on tomatoes, cover with mayonnaise mixed with horse radish and seasoned to taste. Top eggs with pimiento and chives and serve cold.

MARINATED EGGS

6 hard-cooked eggs
½ cup oil
¼ cup vinegar
¼ teaspoon salt, or to taste
¼ teaspoon pepper

2 teaspoons dried oregano
1 teaspoon dried basil
1 teaspoon dried rosemary
½ teaspoon Worcestershire sauce
¼ cup chopped parsley

Slice eggs, cover with marinade made of the next 8 ingredients, refrigerate 8 hours. Dust with parsley and serve with buttered dark bread.

EGGS IN ASPIC I

4 5-minute eggs, cooled and shelled
1 tin liver paté
1 envelope gelatine
¼ cup sherry

1¼ cups bouillon
1 tablespoon tarragon vinegar
salt and pepper to taste
8 tarragon leaves

Empty gelatine into cup, add sherry and set aside 10 minutes. Bring bouillon to boil, take from fire, add gelatine and stir until dissolved, add vinegar and set aside to cool. Divide liver paté over 4 large ramekins or custard cups, press down evenly to make a base, lay an egg into each ramekin. Dip tarragon leaves into liquid aspic and lay 2 crossed leaves on each egg. Pour over aspic when it is cold, but still liquid, and place in refrigerator at least 1 hour.

EGGS IN ASPIC II

4 5-minute eggs, cooled and shelled
4 slices cold tongue, cut julienne
4 truffle slices
1 envelope gelatine
¼ cup sherry

1¼ cups bouillon
salt and pepper to taste
2 tablespoons minced parsley
parsley and gherkins for garnish

Empty gelatine into cup, add sherry and set aside 10 minutes. Bring bouillon to boil, take from fire, add gelatine and stir until dissolved, set aside to cool. Rinse 4 custard or tea cups, pour 1 tablespoon aspic into each and chill until set. Lay a truffle slice into center of each cup, add another tablespoon of aspic and chill again. Place an egg into each cup, pour enough liquid aspic into the cups to come ¾ way up the egg, chill again. If remaining aspic becomes too stiff, set the aspic in its container into a bowl of warm water.

Mix tongue and parsley, press into cups and pour enough aspic over to fill cups. Chill until needed. When ready to serve, dip cups into boiling water and invert onto an aspic- or lettuce-lined platter. Garnish with parsley and gherkins and serve.

EGGS TRUBETZKOI

2 tablespoons butter	4 5-minute eggs
4 thick slices toast	salt and pepper
1 can onion soup	3 tablespoons minced parsley
1 jar hollandaise sauce	

Butter toast, cut into large rounds. Drain onion soup. Place onion on toast rounds, top with peeled eggs and beat remaining soup into stiff hollandaise sauce. Pour over eggs. Season and sprinkle with parsley.

MAJOR EGGS

4 hard-cooked eggs, sliced	salt and freshly ground black
1 can sliced potatoes	pepper
¾ cup heavy sour cream, whipped	½ cup grated horse radish root

Arrange egg and potato slices on serving platter. Season well with salt and pepper. Cover with sour cream whipped with salt and top with horse radish.

SALMON-STUFFED EGGS

4 hard-cooked eggs
2 slices smoked salmon, ground
2 teaspoons grated lemon rind
1 teaspoon minced onion
freshly ground black pepper

4 lettuce leaves
3 tablespoons grated horse radish
½ cup heavy sour cream
salt and pepper

Cut slice from side of each egg. Carefully scoop out yolk and rice it. Mix yolk with ground salmon, rind, onion and enough cream to bind.

Add pepper and refill eggs. Close with slice cut from egg and lay on lettuce leaf, cut side down. Serve with a sauce of sour cream whipped with grated horse radish and salt.

EGGS ALSACE

6 hard-cooked eggs
1 smallest can goose liver paté
½ teaspoon salt
2 teaspoons minced onion

1½ tablespoons mayonnaise
parsley garnish
2 truffles, sliced

Cut eggs in half. Rice yolks with paté, salt, onion and mayonnaise. Season to taste and refill eggs. Garnish each half egg with parsley and a small truffle slice.

MUSTARD-STUFFED EGGS

4 hard-cooked eggs
3 tablespoons mayonnaise
1 tablespoon prepared mustard
½ teaspoon dry mustard
2 tablespoons sweet pickle relish, drained

1 teaspoon minced onion
½ teaspoon salt
paprika
2 sprigs parsley
16 capers

Cut hard-cooked eggs in half, rice yolks, mix with next 6 ingredients. Refill eggs with mixture. Dust with paprika and garnish with a little parsley sprig and capers.

EGG IN BOUILLON

4 cups hot bouillon
4 5-minute eggs
4 tablespoons sherry

2 tablespoons chopped parsley
salt and pepper

Heat bouillon to boiling. Boil eggs exactly 5 minutes, break shells and drop in cold water. Peel carefully and place 1 egg in each cup of bouillon. Add sherry and parsley. Season and serve.

EGGS MIMOSA

4 hard-cooked eggs
¾ cup picked crab meat
¼ cup mayonnaise

1 teaspoon minced onion
salt to taste

Cut eggs in half, rice yolk and set aside. Combine remaining ingredients, refill egg whites and dust generously with riced egg yolk. Crab meat should be entirely covered by yolks.

EGGS AND ASPARAGUS

6 hard-cooked eggs, separated
2 tablespoons oil
1 tablespoon vinegar
1 tablespoon mayonnaise

salt and pepper
2 cans asparagus tips
1 tablespoon grated orange rind
⅔ cup French dressing

Pound yolks with next 4 ingredients, chop whites and add to yolk paste. Mound in the center of a serving dish, surround with drained asparagus spears, dusted with orange rind, and serve French dressing separately.

TUNA-STUFFED EGGS

8 hard-cooked eggs
½ can tuna fish
2 tablespoons oil or to taste

salt and pepper to taste
½ cup chopped parsley

Cut eggs in half, place whites in cold water. Rice egg yolks, mix them with tuna and blend or stir into a smooth paste, add oil and seasonings to taste and fill the egg whites with the mixture. Top mounded filling with parsley and serve on lettuce leaves.

AROMATIC STUFFED EGGS

6 hard-cooked eggs
1 tablespoon Worcestershire sauce
½ teaspoon English mustard
½ teaspoon salt, or to taste
1 tablespoon chopped parsley

1 tablespoon chopped chives
1 tablespoon oil
2 tablespoons mayonnaise
2 tablespoons chopped chives

Cut eggs in half, rice yolks and mix with next five ingredients. Whip in oil and mayonnaise, increase mayonnaise if necessary. Refill egg whites and dust with more chopped chives.

GRECIAN EGGS

4 garlic cloves, crushed
2 egg yolks
salt and freshly ground black
    pepper
½ cup olive oil
3 tablespoons white bread crumbs
3 tablespoons ground almonds

juice of ½ lemon
¼ cup chopped parsley
4 hard-cooked eggs
2 peeled tomatoes
4 sliced radishes
3 tablespoons chopped ripe olives

Stir crushed garlic with egg yolks, season and stir in oil, drop by drop as for mayonnaise. Add crumbs, almonds, lemon juice and parsley and chill. If the sauce separates, stir in one more yolk. Add oil if sauce is too thick. Halve the eggs and lay, round side up, on tomato slices, pour over sauce and top with radishes and olives.

CHAPTER 5.   *Cheese*

C HEESE may not be as old as man, although some people claim it is, but it is certainly as old as man's first milk-producing animals. Man must have discovered very soon that milk would turn sour but that cheese would not only keep indefinitely, but might very easily become as old as some men.

For us, cheese has become a staple food. It is available everywhere, it is nourishing, inexpensive and awfully good. It is an enormous export product from certain countries about which we know very much less than we know about their cheeses.

Cheeses have the great advantage of being good alone, good with fruit, good with pie, good in many combinations and good in the following recipes. These are uncooked cheese recipes, but they are combinations and presentations of cheese which are a little more interesting than the familiar packaged product.

CANADIAN CHEDDAR AND VERMOUTH

¾ cup ground Cheddar   1 tablespoon sweet vermouth
3 tablespoons butter

Beat all ingredients into a smooth paste, fill into crock and chill.

MALAXÉ

¼ pound Roquefort or Blue cheese   1 jigger Calvados (apple brandy)
¼ pound butter

Mix. Spread on buttered black bread and serve.

FRENCH CAMEMBERT WITH PEARS

1 whole ripe Camembert cheese   black bread
½ cup butter   4 ripe pears
¼ pound Gruyere or Swiss cheese
    cut into strips

Cut a circle around the Camembert about ¼ inch from the edge. Lift off this lid and carefully scrape all the cheese into a bowl leaving only the bottom and sides of the cheese. Mash the "lid" with the cheese until it is smooth, add an equal amount of butter, approximately ½ cup, and work the butter and cheese until they are smooth. Refill the shell with the cheese mixture and push spikes of Swiss cheese into the whole surface, like a porcupine. Surround with black bread and serve with pears.

MAYONNAISE AU FROMAGE

6 slices Emmental or Swiss cheese,   salt and pepper to taste
    diced   1 head Boston lettuce
6 large radishes, chopped   6 gherkins
1 chopped onion   2 tablespoons capers
½ cup mayonnaise   1 hard-cooked egg, sliced
1 crushed garlic clove

Mix cheese, radishes and onion, bind with seasoned mayonnaise to which garlic has been added. Line a salad bowl with lettuce, mound the cheese salad in the center and decorate with gherkins, capers and hard-cooked egg.

BLACK AND WHITE BRICK

¼ pound Roquefort cheese   1 package sliced black bread
¼ pound salt butter

Mix cheese and butter into a smooth paste, trim bread and spread it with cheese mixture. Put all layers together, making a brick about 3 inches high, press it with a weight while chilling. Serve sliced very thin.

CHEESE AND TONGUE ROLLS

8 thin slices tongue   ½ teaspoon dry mustard
1 3-ounce package cream cheese   1 tablespoon brandy
3 tablespoons Blue cheese   salt to taste
2 tablespoons butter

Mix cream cheese with next 5 ingredients. Spread tongue slices thinly with the mixture and roll up, starting at the base and ending with the rounded edge of the tongue. Cut each roll in half, trim edges, secure with picks and chill until needed.

SALMON CHEESE ROLLS

3 large or 6 small slices smoked   salt to taste
    salmon   freshly ground black pepper
1 3-ounce package cream cheese   1 lemon, quartered
1 tablespoon sour cream   parsley sprigs
1 tablespoon freshly grated horse
    radish or 2 tablespoons
    bottled horse radish, drained

Mix cheese with cream and horse radish and season to taste. Spread mixture on well-dried salmon slices. Cut slices into strips 1 inch by 3 inches. Dust with freshly ground pepper, roll up, secure with a pick and chill. Serve with lemon wedges and garnish with parsley.

STUFFED MUSHROOMS

18 small, evenly sized, mushrooms
6 tablespoons Roquefort cheese
3 tablespoons butter
1 tablespoon minced onion

½ teaspoon dry mustard
salt to taste
2 tablespoons minced parsley

Remove stems from mushrooms and chop fine. Mix with next 4 ingredients and season to taste. Peel mushroom caps, fill with cheese mixture, dust with parsley and serve.

CREAM CHEESE DIP I

1 8-ounce package cream cheese
4 ounces Blue cheese
2 tablespoons sherry

2 tablespoons mayonnaise
2 tablespoons sour cream
salt to taste

Mix and beat all ingredients until smooth. Increase sour cream if desired. Serve as a dip with potato chips, celery and carrot sticks or raw cauliflower rosettes.

CREAM CHEESE DIP II

½ cup Roquefort cheese
½ cup cream cheese
½ cup sour cream
3 tablespoons ground salted nuts
2 tablespoons minced chives

1 tablespoon minced parsley
1 tablespoon brandy
½ teaspoon dry mustard
salt to taste

Mix all ingredients; thin with additional sour cream if desired. Serve as a dip with potato chips or raw vegetables, celery sticks, carrot sticks or cauliflower rosettes.

FROZEN CHEESE ICE

2 cups heavy cream
¼ cup grated Parmesan

salt, pepper
½ teaspoon paprika

Whip all ingredients together. Pour into ice tray or mold

and freeze in coldest part of refrigerator or in freezer for 3 hours. Unmold and slice with a hot knife, serve with hot buttered toast, and sprinkle with additional Parmesan.

CHEESE-FILLED EGGS

4 hard-cooked eggs
½ cup Cheddar cheese, ground
3 tablespoons butter
salt and pepper to taste
1½ teaspoons capers

4 slices ham
8 gherkins
8 pumpernickel rounds
8 salted almonds
4 parsley sprigs

Cut eggs across lengthwise, rice the yolks and beat them with the cheese and butter into a smooth paste. Season to taste and pipe the mixture back into the egg whites. Decorate each egg with a few capers and place them on shredded lettuce around a flat serving dish. Cut ham slices in half and roll into 8 cornucopias. Lay cut side down into the center of the dish and fill each cornucopia with a gherkin. Spread remaining cheese mixture on the pumpernickel and decorate each round with a salted almond. Arrange the pumpernickel between the stuffed eggs and garnish the dish with parsley.

CREAM CHEESE BALLS I

1 3-ounce package cream cheese
1 tablespoon sour cream
½ tablespoon minced onion
salt to taste

¼ cup toasted sesame seeds
(These may be bought commercially.)

Mix cheese, cream, onion and salt. Form into balls, roll in sesame seeds and chill before serving.

CREAM CHEESE BALLS II

1 3-ounce package cream cheese
1 tablespoon sour cream

½ teaspoon curry powder
¼ cup chopped almonds

Mix cheese, cream and curry powder. Form into balls, roll in chopped almonds and chill before serving.

CREAM CHEESE BALLS III

1 3-ounce package cream cheese
1 tablespoon sour cream

2 tablespoons anchovy paste
3 tablespoons capers, minced

Mix cheese, cream and anchovy paste. Form into balls, roll in minced capers and chill before serving.

CREAM CHEESE BALLS IV

1 3-ounce package cream cheese
1 tablespoon sour cream
1 tablespoon tomato paste

salt to taste
¼ cup chopped chives

Mix cheese, cream, tomato paste and salt. Form into balls, roll in chopped chives and chill before serving.

CREAM CHEESE BALLS V

1 3-ounce package cream cheese
1 tablespoon sour cream
2 tablespoons deviled ham

salt to taste
3 tablespoons minced dill

Mix cheese, cream, deviled ham and salt. Form into balls, roll in minced dill and chill before serving.

WINE CAMEMBERT

1 ripe Camembert
2 cups white wine

½ cup butter
½ cup bread crumbs

Scrape Camembert well, lay into a bowl and cover with wine. Set aside for 12 hours. Drain off wine, add soft butter and blend or work the cheese and butter into a smooth paste, adding a little of the wine if necessary. Shape the cheese into a wedge or round, cover with crumbs and serve.

Cold grapes are lovely with this.

GARNISHED LIPTAUER

1 Camembert cheese
1 Liederkranz cheese
1 8-ounce package cream cheese
4 ounces cottage cheese
¼ cup butter
salt and paprika
1 tablespoon mustard

1 tablespoon sour cream
1 tablespoon paprika, or to taste
1 tablespoon caraway seeds
2 tablespoons minced chives
2 tablespoons minced parsley
2 tablespoons minced onion

Combine cheeses with butter and blend until smooth. Add enough paprika to tint the cheese pink. Form into a mound and set on a cheese board. Surround cheese with little mounds of remaining ingredients. The hostess mixes everything together to taste and guests spread the cheese on buttered black bread. Drink beer with this for a late supper or a Sunday supper.

CHESTER CHEESE AND ALE

1 pound Chester cheese, cut into
    thin slivers
1 tablespoon dry English mustard
2 tablespoons cold water, to taste

English ale to cover
4 slices buttered toast, cut into
    fingers

Place cheese slivers in deep dish. Mix mustard and enough water to obtain a thin smooth mustard. Pour over cheese and add enough ale heated to boiling to just cover cheese and mustard. Serve with buttered toast. Reduce mustard if a milder cheese is preferred.

WHITE WINE, CHEESE AND GRAPES

1 8-ounce package cream cheese
1 package Liederkranz cheese
3 tablespoons white wine
2 teaspoons minced onion

salt to taste
2 pounds seedless grapes or grapes
    in season

Mix first 5 ingredients into a smooth paste. Press into a jar and refrigerate. Serve with chilled grapes and salty crackers.

ROQUEFORT WITH SHERRY

½ pound Roquefort cheese
½ bar or ¼ cup butter, creamed
1 small package cream cheese
¼ cup sherry

1 teaspoon Worcestershire sauce
½ cup cashew nuts, chopped
1 teaspoon paprika
salt to taste

Stir first five ingredients together, shape into a ball and roll in chopped cashew nuts. Serve with crackers or thin buttered bread.

SPICED EDAM CHEESE

1 Edam or Gouda cheese
2 tablespoons prepared mustard

2 tablespoons butter
1 teaspoon paprika

Cut top from Edam or Gouda cheese, scoop out, leaving shell. Mash cheese with prepared mustard, butter and paprika and return to shell. Surround with crackers and serve.

SHARP CHEESE ROLL

1 cup grated American cheese
1 3-ounce package cream cheese
⅓ cup sharp Cheddar cheese, ground
1 garlic clove, crushed

1 teaspoon paprika
1 teaspoon Worcestershire sauce
salt to taste
¾ cup chopped cashew nuts, or pecans

Mix all ingredients except nuts. Shape into a smooth roll about 1½ inches thick. Turn the roll in chopped nuts, wrap in waxed paper and refrigerate. Serve with round crackers and slice cheese roll as needed.

RED CHEESE BALLS

½ cup grated American cheese
1 3-ounce package cream cheese
½ cup chopped walnuts
1 minced pimiento

½ clove garlic, crushed
salt to taste
2 tablespoons paprika
2 sprigs parsley

Mix all ingredients except paprika and parsley. Form into balls, roll in paprika and chill. Insert 1 frill of parsley into each cheese ball with a pointed knife, just before serving.

BLUE CHEESE BALLS

½ cup Blue cheese
1 3-ounce package cream cheese
1 tablespoon sherry
½ tablespoon sour cream

1 teaspoon minced onion
salt to taste
½ cup chopped radishes
4 parsley sprigs

Mix all ingredients except radishes and parsley, form into a ball, roll in chopped radishes and refrigerate until needed. Garnish with parsley sprigs and serve with pumpernickel rounds.

GREEN CHEESE BALLS

1 cup ground sharp Cheddar cheese
1 3-ounce package cream cheese
2 tablespoons brandy

¼ cup ground walnuts
½ teaspoon onion salt
¼ cup finely chopped parsley

Mix all ingredients except parsley and form into marble-sized balls, roll in parsley and chill before serving.

CHEESE CROCKS

Quantities are for ½-pint crocks or jars with covers

BLUE CHEESE AND BRANDY

⅔ cup Blue cheese or Roquefort
3 tablespoons butter

2 tablespoons brandy

Beat all ingredients into a smooth paste, fill into crock and chill.

SHARP CHEDDAR AND SHERRY OR PORT

¾ cup ground sharp Cheddar   2 tablespoons sherry or port
2 tablespoons butter

    Beat all ingredients into a smooth paste, fill into crock and chill.

EDAM AND SAUTERNE

⅔ cup Edam cheese   3 tablespoons Sauterne
3 tablespoons butter

    Beat all ingredients into a smooth paste, fill into crock and chill.

GORGONZOLA AND BRANDY

¾ cup Gorgonzola cheese   1 tablespoon butter
3 tablespoons brandy

    Beat all ingredients into a smooth paste, fill into crock and chill.

STILTON AND PORT WINE

¾ cup Stilton cheese   ¼ cup old port

    Beat all ingredients into a smooth paste, fill into crock and chill.

CHEESE AND TOMATOES

4 peeled tomatoes, sliced
¼ cup French Dressing # 1
    (see page 159)
4 ounces grated cheese
1 tablespoon tomato catsup

¼ cup cream
1 teaspoon grated onion
salt and pepper to taste
1 pinch ground cumin

Marinate tomato slices in French dressing for 30 minutes, drain and arrange on serving dish. Mix next 6 ingredients and spread over tomatoes.

WATER CRESS CHEESE SPREAD

2 8-ounce packages cream cheese
⅔ cup chopped water cress
¼ cup freshly grated or bottled
    horse radish
1 tablespoon sour cream

1 tablespoon mayonnaise
1 teaspoon minced onion
1 teaspoon salt
freshly ground black pepper

Mix and chill. Serve with crackers or salty rye rounds.

CAPER CREAM CHEESE SPREAD

1 8-ounce package cream cheese
3 tablespoons sour cream
2 tablespoons butter
2 tablespoons capers, minced

2 teaspoons paprika
1½ teaspoons onion salt
1 teaspoon prepared mustard
3 tablespoons minced green pepper

Mix first 7 ingredients and serve dusted with minced green pepper. This cheese spread may be used to stuff celery stalks.

ANCHOVY CHEESE SPREAD

1 8-ounce package cream cheese
1 tablespoon anchovy paste
1 tablespoon butter
1 tablespoon sour cream

¼ cup finely chopped walnuts
1 hard-cooked egg, riced
3 tablespoons chopped parsley

Mix first five ingredients, serve chilled with riced hard-cooked egg and parsley topping.

INDIAN SPREAD

1 8-ounce package cream cheese
2 tablespoons minced chutney
1 tablespoon butter

1 tablespoon sour cream
1 teaspoon curry powder
¼ cup crushed coconut chips

Mix first 5 ingredients together, chill and serve dusted with coconut chips.

CHIVE SPREAD

1 8-ounce package cream cheese
2 tablespoons sour cream
½ cup finely chopped chives
1 teaspoon prepared mustard

½ teaspoon salt
freshly ground black pepper to taste
dusting of paprika

Mix all ingredients, chill and serve dusted with paprika. Surround with crackers or pumpernickel rounds.

ZUPPA PAVESE

¼ cup butter
4 slices dry toast
4 eggs, boiled 5 minutes

½ cup grated cheese
3 cups hot bouillon

Butter toast and place slices into 4 wide soup bowls or soup plates. Peel the eggs carefully and lay one on each slice of toast. Dust 2 tablespoons cheese over each egg and add the hot bouillon. Serve at once.

POTATO CHEESE SOUP

2 cans potato soup
1 cup milk
½ cup grated cheese
salt and pepper to taste

½ teaspoon marjoram
1 slice raw potato
¾ cup toasted garlic croutons

Heat soup according to directions on the can, add next 4 ingredients and stir until cheese is melted. Grate the raw potato slice into the soup, stir again and serve hot with croutons.

TOMATO CHEESE SOUP I

2 cans tomato soup
measure 1 can milk
⅔ cup cream, whipped

⅔ cup grated cheese
¼ cup chopped chives
salt and pepper to taste

Mix tomato soup and milk as per directions on can. Heat or chill, according to the season. Whip cream with salt to taste and fold in cheese. Pour soup into 4 plates or cups. Dip a soup spoon into hot water and scoop out egg-shaped portion of whipped cream for each cup. Dust with chives and serve.

TOMATO CHEESE SOUP II

2 cans cream of tomato soup
¼ cup chopped onion
½ garlic clove, crushed
salt and pepper to taste
½ teaspoon sugar
½ teaspoon paprika

½ teaspoon rosemary
1 egg yolk
1 cup grated cheese
1 cup cream
¼ cup chopped parsley

Prepare soup as directed on the can, add next 6 ingredients, stir well and heat. Beat yolk and cheese into cream, take soup from fire and whisk in the mixture. Serve dusted with parsley.

CHAPTER 6. *Breads*

A GREAT deal has been said about the loss of bread baking in the home, about the good effects of kneading dough and the benefits of richer ingredients. No one has said anything about the loss of that lovely smell of bread baking in the oven and the loss of the taste of freshly baked bread. All this might have become a lost art and a lost aroma and taste if it were not being brought back to us by the inventive bakeries who do not want to rob us of all our pleasures. They do all the hard work, they handle the yeast, the kneading and the shaping, and all we have to do is the pleasant part of toasting, heating or finishing it. The oven-ready rolls and biscuits, the sliced breads and the half-baked breads can be sprinkled with herbs or spread with butters and when they go into the toaster or the oven they smell as good, if not as long as home-baked bread used to.

Any of the directions for preparing sliced breads can be applied to brown-and-serve breads, which then require a longer heating time according to the directions on the box. Just plain cold bread and butter should give place to any of the enhanced and embellished varieties that can easily be made without any knowledge of cooking and which make any meal just that much pleasanter.

GARLIC TOAST

Butter hot toast, as it comes out of the toaster, with a mixture of 6 tablespoons creamed butter, 3 crushed garlic cloves and 1 teaspoon dry powdered marjoram. If fresh marjoram is available, use 1½ teaspoons minced instead of dry. This is enough for about 6 toast slices.

CINNAMON TOAST

8 slices white bread	2 tablespoons cinnamon
6 tablespoons soft butter	5 tablespoons brown sugar

Toast bread on one side, butter untoasted side, spread with cinnamon and sugar and toast under broiler until hot.

THE COMPOUNDED BUTTERS

Anchovy Butter:
  cream 2 tablespoons soft butter with ½ inch anchovy paste or ½ teaspoon, chill.

Caviar Butter:
  cream equal parts of soft butter and caviar, chill.

Garlic Butter:
  cream 3 tablespoons soft salt butter with 1 crushed garlic clove, season with salt and chill.

Horse Radish Butter:
  mix freshly grated horse radish, or well-drained bottled horse radish with equal quantities soft salt butter, chill.

Mustard Butter:
  cream 3 tablespoons soft butter with 2 teaspoons prepared mustard, chill.

Paprika Butter:
  stir 3 tablespoons soft salt butter with 1 tablespoon paprika, chill.

Herb Butter:
>   combine minced chives, parsley, chervil or tarragon, according to taste with soft salt butter in following proportions:

2 tablespoons minced mixed herbs	3 tablespoons soft salt butter
1 teaspoon lemon juice	salt and pepper to taste

Curry Butter:
>   cream ¼ cup soft butter with 1 teaspoon curry powder, or to taste, chill.

Catsup Butter:
>   cream ¼ cup soft butter with 2 teaspoons catsup, chill.

CHIVE BREAD

1 small loaf thin white sliced bread	¼ cup minced chives
½ cup soft salt butter	

Spread bread slices with butter, dust with chives. Reshape loaf, wrap lower part of loaf in foil, leaving top open. Place in 375° F oven until bread is hot and butter is bubbling.

ENGLISH MUFFINS

4 English muffins	2 teaspoons garlic salt
6 tablespoons soft butter	3 teaspoons poppy seeds
6 tablespoons grated Parmesan cheese	

Split English muffins with a fork, spread with butter and grated cheese. Dust with garlic salt and poppy seeds. Place under broiler and toast until brown.

TOASTED LOAF

1 loaf sliced white bread	salt
1 package yellow cheese slices	¼ cup soft butter
1 onion sliced thin	

Butter slices lightly. Between slices of bread place ½ slice cheese and 1 onion slice. Reshape loaf, place in a buttered bread pan and heat 15 minutes in a hot 425° F oven.

PARSLEY BREAD

½ loaf sliced white bread	⅓ cup chopped parsley
⅔ cup soft butter	salt

Trim crusts from bread slices and cut in half, butter and dust with parsley. Reshape small loaf of half slices, dust with salt and heat in a 450° F oven for 15 minutes.

ORANGE ROLLS

8 slices white bread	4 tablespoons orange marmalade
4 tablespoons butter	

Trim crusts from bread, butter and spread with marmalade. Roll up, secure with picks and brush with remaining butter. Toast rolls under broiler until brown, turning once. Serve with chicken or duck.

ONION TOAST

8 thin white bread slices	1 teaspoon celery salt
6 tablespoons soft salt butter	4 onion slices divided into rings

Butter bread slices, dust with celery salt, cover with thin onion rings and heat in a 425° F oven for 8 minutes.

POPPY SEED STICKS

4 slices white bread	1 tablespoon poppy seeds
4 tablespoons soft butter	salt

Trim crusts from bread, butter and cut into 3 fingers each.

Spread with poppy seeds and salt and heat in a 425° F oven for 8 minutes or until brown.

TOASTED CORN MUFFINS

4 corn muffins, split
⅓ cup soft butter
3 tablespoons honey

4 tablespoons chopped salted
  pecans
1 tablespoon brown sugar

Butter muffins, brush with honey, spread with pecans and sugar and broil until bubbling.

CHAPTER 7.   *Meat*

SHORT of cannibals and Tartars, most people like their meat cooked; some even like it cooked through. But even the greatest advocate of rare meat wants it to be exposed to heat for a few minutes at least and though he may want a blood-red interior he still wants a hot brown exterior to any meat he eats. So we give you what is called Beefsteak Tartar—some people think of it as Cannibal Steak—the only civilized way we have today of eating raw meat. This is not only civilized, in some of its more elaborate versions, it is a great delicacy, something that no one should miss. Some of the other recipes are for casseroles and meat dishes that only need to be heated and the rest are recipes for cooked meats that can be bought at any supermarket or delicatessen store.

The recipes for using sliced ham and the meats that are referred to as "cold cuts" are all very elaborate; they show what a little effort can do to produce a gala dish for a party out of inexpensive meats that are too often associated with sandwiches and school luncheons. There are directions for making Aspic, the European way of lending enchantment to sliced cold meats. Add an interesting salad and you have a meal that can be prepared in advance and refrigerated until needed.

In spite of the fact that almost all meat is cooked and has no place here, we give you many ways of producing a main course without cooking.

VINEGARED BEEF

3 tablespoons vinegar
3 tablespoons oil
salt, pepper to taste
½ onion, chopped
½ garlic clove, crushed or minced

6 slices cold roast beef
2 tablespoons soft butter
¼ cup tomato paste
1 teaspoon lemon juice
salt, pepper

Combine first 5 ingredients and marinate the roast beef slices in the mixture for at least 2 hours, turning the meat several times. Combine remaining ingredients, arrange the beef with the marinade in a shallow casserole, add the remaining combined ingredients and heat to boiling in a 375° oven. Serve hot with hot crusty bread.

COLD BEEF WITH ORANGES AND POTATO SALAD

2 oranges
½ cup red wine
2 tablespoons brandy
6 slices cold roast beef

¾ cup Sauce Ravigote
(see page 174)
1 white onion sliced paper thin and
divided into rings

1 recipe Potato Salad (see page 146)

Slice oranges thin, remove seeds and marinate in wine and brandy for 2 hours, turning the slices several times. Cut roast beef slices in half. Arrange them on a platter around the oranges and pipe a large rosette of Ravigote Sauce on each slice, or pass the sauce separately. Cover oranges with onion rings and mound potato salad at each end of the platter. Serve as a main dish in summer or as a Sunday night supper in winter.

BEEF TONGUE WITH ORANGES

12 slices cooked beef tongue
¼ cup raisins
¼ cup chopped walnuts
2 tablespoons sugar
2 tablespoons vinegar
½ teaspoon meat glaze or Gravy
    Master

½ cup mayonnaise
salt and pepper to taste
4 oranges
½ cup Basic French Dressing # 2
¼ cup chopped parsley

Stir raisins, walnuts, sugar, vinegar and Gravy Master into mayonnaise and season to taste. Grate the four oranges over a piece of wax paper (see How to Grate Orange Peel) and cut the remaining rind off with a sharp knife so that only the orange meat remains. Retain any juice. Slice the oranges across and arrange them in the center of a platter, pour French Dressing over the oranges and sprinkle with parsley. Surround the oranges with slices of tongue and top with the mayonnaise thinned with any orange juice obtained while cutting the oranges. Sprinkle grated orange rind over mayonnaise sauce and serve as a main course with buttered caraway seed bread.

BEEFSTEAK TARTAR I

2 pounds top round, scraped	1 teaspoon salt, or to taste
(See: How to Scrape Beef.)	2 teaspoons paprika
¼ cup chopped onions	½ teaspoon freshly ground black
3 tablespoons chopped capers	pepper
3 tablespoons prepared mustard	1 egg yolk

Mound scraped beef on a platter garnished with little mounds of onion, capers, mustard, salt, paprika and pepper. Indent top of meat and drop in egg yolk, allow to dry for a few minutes. Surround platter with thinly sliced, buttered pumpernickel bread. Serve by mixing meat with the garnishes and egg yolk and mound on bread or pass separately.

BEEFSTEAK TARTAR II

2-pound slice top round of beef	2 teaspoons paprika
1 onion, chopped	2 tablespoons catsup
3 tablespoons capers	1 egg yolk
2 tablespoons minced dill pickle	salt and pepper to taste
2 tablespoons sherry	black or rye bread and butter

Follow all directions for Beefsteak Tartar # 1, add sherry while mixing meat just before serving.

BEEFSTEAK TARTAR III

2-pound slice top round of beef
½ onion, chopped
4 ounces black caviar
2 egg yolks

1 dash vodka
salt and pepper to taste
1 teaspoon chopped dill, optional
black bread and butter

Follow all directions for Beefsteak Tartar # 1 and serve.

BEEFSTEAK TARTAR IV

1½-pound slice top round of beef
salt and freshly grated black pepper
   to taste
1 large egg yolk

3 tablespoons minced onion
6 chopped anchovy fillets
buttered black bread
1 tablespoon brandy, or to taste

Follow directions for Beefsteak Tartar # 1. Add brandy while mixing meat just before serving.

BEEFSTEAK TARTAR V

2-pound slice beef
3 large dill pickles
1 onion, chopped
4 tablespoons chopped chives

2 teaspoons caraway seeds
salt and pepper to taste
2 egg yolks
black or rye bread and butter

As with all the Beefsteaks Tartar, arrange scraped beef in a round on a platter, make an indentation in the center and drop in the two whole egg yolks. Surround the meat with overlapping slices of dill pickle, mounds of chopped onion and caraway seeds. Sprinkle top with chopped chives and serve. The hostess should stir all ingredients together with freshly ground black pepper and salt to taste and serve the Beefsteak Tartar with bread and butter.

ALOYAU BRETONNE

6 slices cold cooked roast beef,
   diced
2 cans French haricot beans,
   drained

1 can small white onions, drained
1 cup apple cider
salt, pepper
½ cup chopped parsley

Combine first 3 ingredients in the cider in a buttered casserole. Season to taste and heat to boiling in a moderately hot 375° oven. Sprinkle with parsley and serve with French bread and red wine.

HAM AND ASPARAGUS CASSEROLE

2 cans white asparagus
2 cups ground ham
1 cup sour cream

salt, pepper
½ cup grated cheese

Arrange drained asparagus in a shallow buttered casserole and sprinkle with ground ham. Mix cream and cheese and season to taste, pour over ham and heat to boiling in a moderately hot 375° F oven. Serve at once.

BEEF TONGUE CASSEROLE

¼ cup small raisins
½ cup red wine
12 slices cooked beef tongue
½ cup red currant jelly

½ cup slivered blanched almonds
2 oranges, juice and grated rind
1 lemon, juice and grated rind
salt, pepper

Soak the raisins in the red wine for an hour. Arrange the sliced tongue in a low buttered casserole and cover with remaining ingredients. Add raisins and wine and heat the casserole in a moderately hot oven 375° F until it reaches the boiling point. Serve hot.

BEEF STEW

½ clove garlic, minced
2 cans beef stew
1 can small white onions, drained
1 can small potatoes, drained

1 can button mushrooms, drained
salt, pepper
½ cup red wine, or to taste
1 tablespoon brandy

Combine first 5 ingredients and season to taste. Add red wine, increasing quantity to taste, and heat in a moderately hot 375°

oven. Add brandy and serve very hot. Canned rice or spaghetti may be heated and served as a side dish, or serve it with hot crusty bread and butter.

BEEF AND CAVIAR

4 thick slices rare cold roast beef
7 ounces Russian caviar
    (called ½ pound)
1 jar frozen Béarnaise sauce

4 canned cooked artichoke bottoms
4 sprigs parsley
1 lemon, quartered
fingers of buttered black bread

Trim beef slices and spread with caviar. Pipe Béarnaise sauce into artichoke bottoms. Arrange beef on a serving platter with artichoke bottoms and lemon wedges. Garnish with parsley and serve chilled.

FRENCH BEEF SALAD

1½ cups diced cooked beef
1 onion, chopped
1 can sliced potatoes
2 tablespoons chopped chives
2 tablespoons chopped parsley
1 teaspoon capers
1 teaspoon salt

¼ teaspoon pepper
½ cup French dressing
½ cup mayonnaise
½ head Boston lettuce
1 dill pickle, sliced
1 hard-cooked egg, sliced

Combine first 8 ingredients and add a mixture of dressing and mayonnaise. Arrange salad on lettuce leaves on a serving platter and cover with pickle and egg slices.

ASPIC FOR MEAT DISHES

As the making of aspic only requires bringing the liquid to a boil, and as the use of aspic enhances many cold dishes, it is included here.

One envelope plain gelatine will "set" 1 quart liquid. The following recipe calls for only ½ pint of liquid because the aspic will set faster, because it will not melt as easily and because it will be used as a garnish or glaze rather than as a jelly or mousse.

> 1 envelope plain gelatine
> 1/4 cup cold wine or water
> 1 cup or can bouillon or consommé
> 1 onion slice, optional
> salt and pepper to taste
> 2 tablespoons wine to brush or sprinkle
> on finished aspic

Empty gelatine into a cup or measuring cup. Pour cold wine or water over gelatine and set aside to soften. In the meantime, heat bouillon to boiling, take from heat and stir in the lump of softened gelatine until it is dissolved or pour boiling bouillon over the gelatine and stir until dissolved. Onion may be placed in the cold bouillon and removed after the bouillon has come to a boil, before the gelatine is added.

Diced Aspic: When gelatine is dissolved, pour the liquid aspic into a cold bowl, let it cool and set in refrigerator to chill. Scoop out pieces of stiff aspic, lay on paper and chop for use as a garnish. Moisten with a little wine to enhance its gloss. Allow 2 hours for chilling and setting.

Cubed Aspic: When gelatine is dissolved, pour liquid aspic into a shallow pan so that the aspic is from 1/4 to 1/2 inch deep, cool and chill. Invert sheet of gelatine onto a piece of paper and cut with a silver knife into 1/4 or 1/2 inch cubes. Moisten with a little wine to enhance gloss. Allow 2 hours for chilling and setting.

Aspic "Mirror" for Platter or Serving Dish: This is recommended for egg dishes which often turn silver black and for enhancing cold meat and buffet platters. Pour liquid aspic into the platter or serving dish that is to be used. Make enough aspic so that the layer is from 1/8 to 1/4 inch deep. Let aspic cool, then transfer the platter to refrigerator and chill for 45 minutes until aspic is set. Brush aspic with wine and arrange the food on the aspic, garnish and return to refrigerator until it is served.

Aspic for Glazing: When gelatine is dissolved pour it into a cup and set aside to cool. Place in refrigerator until it thickens slightly but is still liquid enough to flow. It should have the consistency of heavy oil. If aspic were to "set" before glazing is completed, place cup of aspic into bowl of tepid water until aspic is liquid again. Glaze the meat or other food by brushing on the aspic with a wide pastry brush. Set the glazed food in the refrigerator and keep the aspic at room temperature. Repeat brushing and chilling until a heavy, glossy coat of aspic is obtained. The first and second coats will hardly show, but after that the aspic will go on smoothly. If the food to be glazed is smooth or flat, and aspic will not run off, heavier coats may be poured on instead of being brushed on.

Glazing a Mold with Aspic: There are 2 methods of glazing a mold.

1. Pour a little cooled aspic that has reached the consistency of heavy oil, into a chilled mold and tilt the mold in such a way that all surfaces are coated with a thin film of aspic. Chill the mold and repeat until the mold is evenly glazed. The aspic may also be brushed on as for glazing meat.

2. Fill a chilled, rinsed mold with liquid aspic and set in refrigerator. As soon as a layer of aspic has "set" on the mold, pour off the liquid aspic and chill the glazed mold. Any decorations or cut outs should be dipped in liquid aspic and held against the glazed walls of the mold until they adhere. Fill mold as recipe requires and chill until needed.

    To unmold an aspic: Dip mold into boiling water for 1 instant and invert onto a serving platter.

    Avoid using red beets in aspics as the red color bleeds into the aspic.

PLAIN MEAT SALAD

2 cups diced cold ham, beef, veal and/or pork	salt and pepper
1 cup diced canned potatoes	½ cup thick mayonnaise
½ cup diced dill pickle	1 tablespoon prepared mustard
¼ cup French Dressing # 2	lettuce leaves
	4 parsley sprigs

Combine first 3 ingredients, bind with dressing and season to taste, chill. Before serving fold in mayonnaise stirred with mustard and arrange the meat salad on lettuce leaves in a salad bowl. Garnish wih parsley and serve.

Variation: Less Plain Meat Salad. To above salad add 2 hard-cooked eggs, sliced and garnish with 1 can well-drained rolled anchovies.

COLD PORK AND APPLES

6 slices cold roast pork
6 slices liverwurst, skinned
2 hard-cooked eggs, sliced
2 tablespoons chopped parsley
2 tablespoons chopped onion
salt and pepper

1 jar stewed apple slices
½ teaspoon cinnamon
juice and shredded rind of 1 orange
juice of 1 lemon
½ cup red currant jelly, melted

Arrange cold pork on serving platter, top each slice with a slice of liverwurst and 2 slices hard-cooked egg. Garnish with chopped onion and parsley. Surround meat with well-drained apples and pour a sauce over apples made of melted jelly mixed with orange, lemon and cinnamon. Pass whipped mayonnaise separately.

MINTED COLD PORK

1 envelope gelatine
¼ cup water or bouillon
1 cup mint sauce
8 slices cold pork roast
salt and pepper to taste

1 can tiny green peas
¼ cup French Dressing # 1
2 tablespoons heavy cream
4 mint sprigs

Soften gelatine in water or bouillon, heat mint sauce, take from fire, add gelatine and stir until dissolved, correct seasoning. Cool sauce, arrange sliced pork on shallow platter, pour sauce over pork when it starts to set. Mix green peas with dressing and cream. Mound peas in center of platter and garnish with mint sprigs.

PINEAPPLE PORK

8 slices cold roast pork
1 crushed garlic clove
½ cup mayonnaise
8 slices canned pineapple
1 can chicken liver paté

3 tablespoons chopped parsley
salt and pepper
2 tablespoons melted currant jelly
2 tablespoons sherry

Add garlic to mayonnaise and whip with 2 or 3 tablespoons pineapple juice into a thin sauce. Season and coat meat with sauce, top each slice with a pineapple slice and center with a ball of paté rolled in chopped parsley. Mix jelly and sherry and cool until thick. Pour a little around each pineapple slice and serve.

COLD HAM VINAIGRETTE

1½ pounds sliced ham
1 teaspoon salt
1 sliver garlic, crushed
½ teaspoon roughly ground black
    pepper
6 tablespoons tarragon vinegar
1 teaspoon lemon juice
1 cup olive oil

2 tablespoons chopped onion
2 tablespoons chopped capers
2 tablespoons chopped parsley
1 riced hard-cooked egg
2 cans white asparagus
2 dill pickles
mustard

Stir salt, garlic and pepper with a wooden spoon in a bowl, with a "crushing" motion, moisten with vinegar, lemon juice and stir in oil slowly. Add onion, capers and parsley, pouring into a bottle and shake well. Arrange cold sliced ham on serving platter, place drained asparagus at either end. Add riced egg to vinaigrette and pour over asparagus. Garnish platter with dill pickle cut into 1-inch rounds, scooped out slightly and filled with prepared mustard.

HAM TOMATOES

4 large peeled tomatoes
1 cup chopped cooked ham
1 hard-cooked egg, chopped
¼ cup finely chopped celery
1 small avocado, diced

2 tablespoons chopped dill pickle
¼ cup French Dressing # 2
salt and pepper
½ head Boston lettuce

Cut lids off tomatoes, carefully scoop out pulp and drain shells. Mix next five ingredients, season to taste and blend with a little French dressing. Fill into tomatoes and chill. Serve on lettuce leaves and pass sauce separately:

>1 cup mayonnaise
>1 tablespoon tomato paste
>1 sliver garlic clove, crushed
>¼ cup chopped chives
>salt and pepper

Mix ingredients and serve.

HAM MOUSSE
for 6

3 cups ground cooked ham
2 envelopes gelatine
⅓ cup sherry
½ cup boiling water
2 teaspoons prepared mustard

2 tablespoons grated horse radish
salt, pepper and cayenne
2 eggs, separated
1 cup heavy cream, whipped

Empty gelatine in a measuring cup, add sherry and set aside for 10 minutes. Add boiling water and stir until dissolved. Stir into ground ham with mustard, horse radish and egg yolks and season to taste. Whip cream, beat egg whites stiff and fold both into ham mixture. Pour mixture into a rinsed soufflé dish or mold and chill until set. Unmold and serve with mustard sauce, or curry sauce. If mousse is a buffet or dinner main dish, it can be surrounded with stuffed eggs.

BASQUE HAM BREAD

1 round loaf rye or pumpernickel
    bread
2 cans liver paté
1 onion, chopped
2 garlic cloves, crushed
5 large tomatoes, peeled, seeded,
    drained and chopped

1 green pepper, seeded and
    chopped
4 hard-cooked eggs, sliced
¼ cup chopped parsley
6 thick slices cooked ham, cut
    julienne
salt and pepper

French Dressing #2

Cut slice from top of day-old rye bread and hollow out interior completely. Spread inside and lid of loaf with liver paté, mixed with a little butter if it is too dry to spread easily. Fill loaf with a mixture of remaining ingredients, seasoned to taste. Replace lid and serve immediately as a luncheon dish. Each guest is served with a wedge of the bread and a portion of the filling. If preferred, the dressing can be omitted from the filling and passed separately.

STUFFED MUSHROOMS

8 large mushrooms
½ cup French Dressing # 2
1 cup ground ham
1 teaspoon soy sauce

1 tablespoon minced onion
salt and pepper
1 pinch ground ginger
¼ cup toasted sesame seeds

Carefully remove mushroom stems and chop. Clean caps with a cloth and brush with French dressing, leaving a spoon of dressing in each mushroom to marinate for ½ hour. In the meantime, mix ham with chopped stems and all other ingredients, except sesame seed, and season to taste. Fill ham into drained mushroom caps, mounding the center and roll stuffed side down in sesame seeds. Serve on lettuce leaves with remaining dressing poured over lettuce.

HAM AND EGGS

½ cup soft butter
2 teaspoons prepared mustard
1 teaspoon dry mustard
salt, pepper and cayenne
2 tablespoons chopped chutney
2 tablespoons grated horse radish
1 tablespoon tarragon vinegar

juice of 2 limes
salt and pepper
4 thick slices cooked ham
4 5-minute eggs, cooled and peeled
3 tablespoons chopped chives
1 lime, quartered

Cream butter until very light, beat in next 7 ingredients, season to taste and chill a few minutes. Arrange ham slices on serving platter, pipe a circle of the butter on each slice and lay a cold egg into the circle, dust with chives, garnish with lime quarters and serve with black bread.

HAM CORNETS

8 slices cooked ham
12-ounce section liverwurst
3 tablespoons soft butter
1 tablespoon mayonnaise
8 black olives, pitted and chopped
salt and freshly ground black
    pepper
1 pinch cayenne

3 tablespoons chopped pistachio
    nuts or parsley
1 envelope gelatine
1/3 cup sherry
4 small tomatoes, peeled, scooped
    out and drained
1 cup mayonnaise
3 tablespoons chopped parsley

3 tablespoons chopped pecans

Rice or blend liverwurst with next 5 ingredients. Roll ham slices into cornucopias, or if cornet molds are available, line them with ham slices. Pipe liverwurst paté into the cornets and decorate the open end with chopped pistachio nuts or chopped parsley. Chill the cornets until ready to serve. In the meantime empty gelatine into a measuring cup, add sherry and set aside for 10 minutes. Heat jellied chicken consommé to boiling, take from heat immediately and stir in gelatine until it dissolves. Pour consommé into a shallow pan so that it is 1/4 inch deep. Cool and chill.

When ready to serve, cut gelatine into 1/4-inch dice with knife, arrange in center of a lettuce-lined platter, surround with ham cornets and the tomatoes filled with mayonnaise. Dust parsley and pecans over aspic jelly and serve as a luncheon dish.

TONGUE AND MUSHROOMS

8 slices cold boiled tongue
2 cups sliced mushrooms
1/2 cup French Dressing # 1
1/2 crushed garlic clove

3 tablespoons minced onion
3 tablespoons chopped chives
lettuce leaves

Cut tongue into julienne strips. Pour dressing over mushrooms, add remaining ingredients and marinate 1 hour. Serve mushrooms on lettuce leaves, topped with tongue, and accompany each portion with thin buttered rye bread.

FRANKFURT MEAT SALAD

6 frankfurters, skinned and sliced
    thin
⅔ cup oil
⅓ cup tarragon vinegar
1 sliced onion
4 sprigs parsley, stems removed

1 tablespoon prepared mustard
½ teaspoon dry mustard
1 teaspoon paprika
1 teaspoon sugar
1 to 2 teaspoons salt
black pepper to taste

Blend all ingredients, except frankfurters, to a thick sauce. Add frankfurters and pour over green salad, bean or potato salad. Sauce can be thinned with more oil if desired.

TONGUE AND SPINACH

8 slices cold boiled tongue
½ cup grated horse radish
½ cup whipped cream
salt and pepper

1 pound washed, dry spinach leaves
½ cup French Dressing # 3
2 peeled sliced tomatoes

Roll tongue into cornucopias, fill with horse radish mixed with seasoned whipped cream, and arrange on platter. Add mound of spinach salad. Pour dressing over the spinach. Serve with sliced tomatoes and accompany each portion with thin buttered black bread.

CHAPTER 8.   *Poultry*

Tʜᴇsᴇ recipes for hot and cold poultry only require mixing, heating or chilling and serving. As in the other chapters, some of the ingredients have to be minced or chopped but that is the worst that can happen to you. This does not mean that the recipes call for "One can chicken combined with one can mushrooms and one tablespoon chopped parsley." It means 35 ways of serving a meal, summer or winter, with a main course that can never take more than about 20 minutes to prepare.

Some of the recipes call for a casserole and a hot oven to heat it in, but none of the ingredients can be harmed by over- or under-heating. There are no chickens which have to be cooked and none submerged in heavy combinations of butter and flour.

It means new and interesting chicken dishes, easily arrived at, and new menu making, also simply arrived at. All the forms of chicken suggested in the recipes can be bought at delicatessen stores or in cans. Sliced chicken or sliced turkey can be bought at all meat counters today, and all recipes for sliced or minced chicken can be used for sliced or minced turkey.

ITALIAN CHICKEN CASSEROLE

2 cups cooked or canned chicken
    cut in large pieces
1 can cream of mushroom soup
½ cup cream
3 tablespoons sherry

1 can sliced mushrooms, drained
salt and pepper
1 jar cooked spaghetti or macaroni
    without sauce
3 tablespoons Parmesan

Combine first 5 ingredients, season to taste and mound them in center of a shallow casserole. Surround with a border of spaghetti or macaroni and sprinkle with Parmesan. Heat to boiling in a moderately hot 375° F oven and serve at once.

CHICKEN AND ALMONDS

3 cups diced cooked or canned
    chicken
1 cup scalded, chopped almonds
1 can cream of celery soup
¼ teaspoon sage

2 tablespoons sherry
½ cup or 1 can green seedless
    grapes
salt, pepper
2 tablespoons chopped parsley

Combine first 6 ingredients in a buttered casserole, season to taste and heat through in a moderately hot 375° F oven. Serve sprinkled with parsley.

CHICKEN CASSEROLE

1½ cups cooked or canned diced
    chicken
1 can cream of chicken soup
1 can baby lima beans, drained

1 can button mushrooms, drained
3 tablespoons sherry, or to taste
salt, pepper
3 tablespoons Parmesan

Combine first 5 ingredients in a shallow buttered casserole, season to taste and sprinkle with Parmesan. Heat through in a moderately hot 375° F oven and serve immediately.

CHICKEN STEW

1½ pounds cooked or canned
    chicken cut into chunks
1 can small white onions, drained
½ can carrots and peas, drained
1 can cream of chicken soup
1 teaspoon oregano

salt, pepper
heavy cream to taste
2 hard-cooked eggs, sliced
1 cup toasted garlic flavored bread
    croutons
3 tablespoons chopped parsley

Combine first 5 ingredients in a shallow buttered casserole, season to taste and thin with cream to desired consistency. Add sliced eggs carefully so that they remain intact and heat to boiling in a moderately hot 375° F oven. Top with croutons, sprinkle with parsley and serve.

GOTEBORG PATÉ

1 can chicken liver paté
1 3-ounce package cream cheese
2 tablespoons sherry
1 tablespoon mayonnaise

2 chopped truffles
1 tablespoon minced onion
1 tablespoon minced parsley
salt, pepper and cayenne

Mix all ingredients, roll in waxed paper and chill. Serve cut in slices on toast rounds of the same size as the paté rounds. Serve as a luncheon dish topped with chopped aspic.

BRUGES CHICKEN SALAD

2 cups diced cooked chicken
1 can sliced potatoes, diced
1 cup diced celery
½ cup finely diced raw cauliflower
1 cup chopped onion
    ¼ cup chopped parsley or chives

6 slices bacon, cut into small dice
    with scissors
1 teaspoon caraway seeds
¼ cup tarragon vinegar
salt and pepper to taste

Combine first 5 ingredients and set aside. Heat bacon in pan to sizzling, or until bacon dice are browned. Add caraway and vinegar. Pour over salad, season to taste, dust with parsley or chives, and serve at once or cool before serving.

CHICKEN OLGA

4 slices thick ham
4 Suprêmes of chicken (see
    Chicken Jeanette)
2 envelopes gelatine

½ cup port wine
1 cup mayonnaise
1 cup cream of chicken soup,
    strained

Follow recipe for Chicken Jeanette. Soften gelatine in port wine, dissolve in boiling chicken soup and cool. Dress chicken on ham slices, add well-beaten mayonnaise to gelatine mixture and spread over Suprêmes. Chill and lay Suprêmes around a salad of green peas and serve as a main dish, at dinner or buffet.

COLD CHICKEN JEANETTE

2 envelopes gelatine
1 can chicken consommé
1 can cream of chicken soup
2 cold cooked broilers

4 thick slices ham
1 can goose liver paté
2 truffles
8 tarragon leaves

Empty gelatine into a cup, add ½ cup consommé, and set aside, heat remaining consommé to boiling and pour over gelatine. Stir until dissolved. Cool and add well-beaten and strained cream soup; cool, but do not allow to set. Carve 4 breasts with wings attached from chickens, draw off skins and use remaining chicken for salad or mousse. Dress the breasts (called Suprêmes) on ham trimmed to size of Suprêmes and spread with goose liver paté. Place on wire mesh or broiler grill and pour a thin layer of gelatine over them. Chill and repeat until Suprêmes are beautifully coated. Keep gelatine soft enough to spread by placing over tepid water. Trim tops with sliced truffles and crossed tarragon leaves. Serve very cold as a main dish at dinner with hot vegetables or at a buffet.

TURKISH CHICKEN

1½ cups diced canned chicken
1 can boiled rice
½ cup diced celery
1 can button mushrooms
¼ cup chopped black olives
¾ cup green grapes, pitted or
    seedless

2 cups shredded lettuce
1 teaspoon salt
¼ teaspoon pepper
¼ teaspoon rosemary
2 teaspoons onion juice
4 tablespoons vinegar
8 tablespoons oil

Combine first 6 ingredients, place on shredded lettuce on a crystal serving dish. Mix or shake next 6 ingredients and pour over chicken. Serve very cold.

CHICKEN LIVERS GIGI

1 can chicken liver paté
2 slices ham, slivered
4 hard-cooked eggs
¼ cup chopped onion

1½ cups shredded lettuce
⅔ cup French Dressing # 1
4 truffle slices

Arrange shredded lettuce in a ring on 4 salad plates. Place hard-cooked egg, sliced but kept in its original shape, into nest of lettuce. Cover with slivered ham mixed with chopped onion. Pour over dressing and rice ¼ can of chicken liver paté over each portion. Center with a truffle slice and serve with toast fingers.

CHICKEN JULIANNA

2 cups shredded lettuce
2 cups cold chicken, cut julienne
6 slices tongue, cut julienne
2 slices Swiss cheese, cut julienne
1 outside orange peel, cut julienne

1 outside lemon peel, cut julienne
1 cup mayonnaise
2 tablespoons lemon juice
1 tablespoon chili sauce

Mound lettuce in center of serving dish. Cover with next 5 ingredients. Combine mayonnaise with lemon juice and chili sauce and pour over julienne. Top with sections cut from the peeled orange and serve very cold.

CHICKEN AND ASPARAGUS

1 envelope gelatine
1 can chicken consommé
1 cold cooked chicken, quartered
2 cans white asparagus

1 cup mayonnaise
1 teaspoon paprika
3 tablespoons chopped chives
salt and pepper

Empty gelatine into cup, add ¼ can consommé. Heat remaining consommé to boiling, pour over gelatine and stir until dissolved. Cool and set in refrigerator to chill for 2 hours.

Arrange chicken and asparagus on serving platter. Chop aspic into neat dice and arrange around chicken. Mix mayonnaise with paprika and chives, season and pass separately.

CHICKEN CAESAR

1 cold roast broiler, quartered
½ pound sliced mushrooms
½ cup French dressing
1 crushed garlic clove
2 tablespoons minced onion
2 tablespoons minced chives

2 tablespoons brandy
¾ cup sour cream
1 lemon, juice and grated rind
salt and pepper
1 head Boston lettuce

Marinate mushrooms in dressing with next 3 ingredients 1 hour. Arrange quartered broiler on serving platter. Center with mushroom salad arranged in a cup of lettuce leaves. Mix brandy into sour cream, add lemon juice and rind and season well. Chill and pass with chicken.

CHICKEN AND LIVER RICE

1 can wild rice
1 can sliced mushrooms
1 cup cooked or canned chicken
1 can cream of chicken soup

salt and pepper
1 can chicken liver paté
3 tablespoons chopped parsley

Combine first 4 ingredients in a buttered casserole, season to taste and heat to bubbling in a moderate 350° oven. Rice paté over top of casserole, dust with parsley and return to oven for 5 minutes. Serve with "Brown and Serve" French bread, generously buttered, and a green salad.

LIVER PATÉ LIANA

2 cans chicken liver paté
2 tablespoons butter
salt and pepper
¼ teaspoon ground mace
¼ cup shelled pistachio nuts

1 tablespoon minced onion
5 tablespoons mayonnaise
2 tablespoons brandy
1 hard-cooked egg, separated
½ cup minced parsley

Combine first 8 ingredients, add riced egg yolk and set aside egg white. Shape into rounds and roll in parsley. Serve on lettuce leaves topped with riced egg white.

Serve hot garlic bread or rolls with these as a luncheon dish. Serve as a first course for dinner or with cocktails.

CHICKEN TOASTS

1 cup ground cooked chicken
salt and pepper to taste
2 tablespoons chili sauce
½ can chicken liver paté
1 hard-cooked egg

2 tablespoons minced parsley
4 slices buttered toast, cut into 3
   fingers each
¼ head Boston lettuce

Mix first 3 ingredients and spread on toast. Arrange 3 fingers each on lettuce leaves on 4 luncheon plates. Rice a little liver paté over each finger and rice egg over the paté. Top with chopped parsley and serve with a mixed fruit salad for luncheon or serve as a first course at dinner.

CHICKEN LIVER PATÉ IN CUCUMBERS

2 cans chicken liver paté
3 small or 2 large cucumbers
1 tablespoon salt

4 tablespoons chopped chives
1 cup diced aspic (see Aspic)
2 tablespoons sherry

Score cucumbers with a ridged knife, or peel. Cut off both ends and hollow out with sharp knife or apple corer. Lay hollowed cucumbers in salted ice water for 1 hour. Dry well and fill with chicken liver paté. Chill for at least 1 hour. Cut cucumbers in ¾-inch slices, arrange on luncheon plates, top with chives and garnish with diced aspic, moistened with a little sherry.

Serve with buttered hot rolls.

CHICKEN SALAD

1½ cups cold cooked or canned chicken, cubed
½ cup diced celery
¾ cup diced apple
½ cup seedless grapes, optional
½ teaspoon salt
¼ teaspoon pepper
½ cup mayonnaise
1 large cantaloupe
2 tablespoons chopped parsley
lettuce leaves

Mix first 7 ingredients. Cut ends off cantaloupe, remove seeds and cut remaining melon into 4 thick slices, making hollow rings. Lay rings on lettuce leaves on 4 plates. Fill with chicken salad and dust with parsley.

COLD CHICKEN ROSSINI

2 envelopes gelatine
½ cup sherry
1½ cups clear chicken consommé
salt and pepper
1 cup mayonnaise
1 can goose liver paté
1 large jar cooked chicken
2 truffles
1 peeled tomato
parsley for garnish

Empty gelatine into a cup, add sherry and set aside. Bring consommé to boiling, take from heat and stir in lump of softened gelatine until it is dissolved, season to taste and set aside to cool. When consommé is cooled, but before it has started to set, fold in mayonnaise. Divide goose liver paté into 4 portions, arrange on a small serving platter, cover each portion with slices of chicken and pour the aspic-mayonnaise over the entire platter.

Place 2 or 3 truffle slices on each mound of chicken and chill. To serve, slice tomato, cut slices in half and lay the half-rounds along the edge of the platter. Garnish with parsley and serve with a green salad.

COLD CHICKEN CERNY

1 envelope gelatine
1½ cups chicken consommé
1 cup heavy cream
2 tablespoons minced parsley
1 tablespoon minced chives
2 tablespoons minced spinach
1 teaspoon minced onion

½ cup soft salt butter
4 thick slices cold boiled tongue
1 whole canned chicken, quartered
2 cans green asparagus spears
½ cup mayonnaise
salt and pepper
parsley for garnish

Empty gelatine into a cup, add ¼ cup of the consommé, heat remaining consommé to boiling, take from heat and stir in gelatine until it is dissolved. Cool for 10 minutes, stir in ½ cup of the cream and set aside. Stir parsley, chives, spinach and onion into butter. Spread the butter on tongue slices, cover with chicken quarters and arrange on a small serving platter. Pour the cooled aspic sauce over the chicken and chill. Whip the cream, fold into mayonnaise, season and chill. To serve, lay the drained asparagus between the portions of chicken and serve with the whipped cream sauce. Garnish with parsley.

CHERRY CHICKEN SALAD

1½ cups cold, cooked chicken
1 can button mushrooms
1 can asparagus tips, drained
1 cup pineapple chunks, drained

¾ cup French Dressing # 1
2 tablespoons mayonnaise
1 cup fresh or canned red
   cherries, pitted

Combine first 4 ingredients with dressing and mayonnaise, mound on serving platter and top with cherries. Serve with buttered black bread slices.

COLD PORTUGUESE CHICKEN

16 cooked shrimps, halved
   lengthwise
1½ cups diced cooked chicken
   meat
2 teaspoons lemon juice

2 tablespoons port wine
2 large tomatoes, peeled
½ cup mayonnaise, or to taste
4 lettuce leaves
salt and pepper to taste

Mix shrimps and chicken with lemon juice and port wine and refrigerate 1 hour. Bind with mayonnaise and serve on 4 lettuce leaves with 2 thick slices of tomato on each serving.

PLAIN CHICKEN SALAD

2 cups cold or canned chicken, cut into strips
1 cup peeled and cored apples, cut into strips
½ cup seeded cucumbers, cut into strips

¼ cup Lemon Dressing (see page 162)
salt and pepper
½ cup mayonnaise
1 teaspoon prepared mustard
3 tablespoons chopped chives
lettuce leaves

Combine first 3 ingredients, bind with dressing, and season to taste, chill. Before serving, fold in mayonnaise stirred with mustard and arrange the chicken salad on lettuce leaves in a salad bowl. Dust with chives and serve.

Variation: To above salad add 4 slices smoked tongue, cut into strips, and surround with 2 peeled and sliced tomatoes.

ARTICHOKE AND CHICKEN SALAD

2 cups diced cold cooked chicken meat
12 canned artichoke hearts, drained
shredded lettuce
½ clove garlic
1 cup mayonnaise
4 anchovy fillets, diced

1 tablespoon minced onion
2 teaspoons chopped parsley
2 teaspoons chopped chives
2 teaspoons chopped tarragon
1 tablespoon tarragon vinegar
salt and pepper

Arrange 3 artichoke hearts each on 4 beds of shredded lettuce on 4 salad plates. Rub a small bowl with cut side of garlic clove, mix mayonnaise in the bowl with chicken and all remaining ingredients and mound chicken salad on artichoke hearts. Serve chilled as a luncheon salad.

POULTRY [125

COLD CHICKEN SOUFFLÉ

1 envelope gelatine
¼ cup water or consommé
1 can cream of chicken soup
1 tablespoon curry powder, or to
   taste
2 cups ground chicken

1 cup cream, whipped
salt and pepper
1 cup chutney
2 slices tongue, cut into rounds
2 slices cold chicken, cut into
   rounds

Empty gelatine into cup, add water or consommé and set aside. Bring chicken soup to boiling, pour over gelatine and stir until dissolved, add curry powder and continue to stir until smooth. Add chicken and set aside to cool. Fold in whipped cream, season and pour mixture into a soufflé dish. Place a glass or cup in center and chill. Remove cup and fill cavity with chutney and cover with tongue and chicken disks, cut with smallest cookie cutter.

CHICKEN IN CASSEROLE

1 whole canned or roasted chicken.
salt and pepper

1 can condensed cream of chicken
   soup

Quarter chicken, place in buttered casserole with soup, season. Cover and heat to bubbling in a 375° F oven.

Variations:
1. Dust with 1 riced hard-cooked egg and 3 tablespoons chopped parsley just before serving.
2. Add 2 cans button mushrooms to casserole.
3. Add 1 can drained okra to casserole.
4. Add 1 can drained tomatoes and ½ teaspoon each oregano and basil to casserole.

COLD CHICKEN ISABELLA

2 cups mayonnaise
1 teaspoon paprika
salt and pepper
2 cups cold boiled rice
1 pimiento, diced

8 slices cold breast of chicken
3 tablespoons chopped chives or
   parsley
1 can green asparagus tips
1 lemon, thinly sliced

Beat mayonnaise with paprika, use half of it to bind well-seasoned rice. Add pimiento to rice and mound in center of serving platter. Lay chicken slices over rice spread with remaining mayonnaise and sprinkle with chives. Arrange asparagus tips at either end of platter and garnish with lemon slices.

MINCED CHICKEN NESTS

2 cups minced cooked chicken	4 5-minute eggs
1 can condensed cream of chicken soup	1 can sliced mushrooms
	salt and pepper

Boil eggs, crack shells and set aside in warm water. Bring soup to boiling, stirring constantly; add half of it, little by little, to the chicken to form a thick purée. Return to heat and stir until chicken is hot, arrange chicken on 4 plates in a circle or nest. Peel warm eggs and lay 1 in the center of each nest. Add mushrooms and their liquor to remaining chicken soup, season, thin with cream if necessary, heat to boiling and pour over eggs. Serve at once.

FRICASSEE

2 cans chicken fricassee	salt and pepper
1 can white potatoes	½ cup heavy cream, or to taste
1 can white onions	2 hard-cooked eggs, sliced
1 small can whole carrots	4 slices thick toast

Heat first 4 ingredients to boiling, season well and add cream. Heat again, pour into a hot serving dish, top with egg slices and surround with toast triangles.

COLD CHIVED CHICKEN RING

1 envelope gelatine	1 cup cream, whipped
¼ cup water or bouillon	2 cans tiny lima beans, drained
1 cup chive sauce	¼ cup French Dressing # 1
2 cups cold ground chicken	parsley sprigs
salt and pepper to taste	

Soften gelatine in water or bouillon, heat chive sauce (a cream sauce in which half the liquid is chicken stock, fortified by 1½ tablespoons chives per cup), take from fire, add gelatine; stir until dissolved, correct seasoning. Mix sauce with chicken, fold in whipped cream, pour into a rinsed ring mold. Cool; chill. Mix lima beans with dressing. Unmold chicken ring, fill center with beans. Garnish with parsley.

COLD CHICKEN CURRY

1 envelope gelatine
¼ cup water
½ cup orange juice
1½ cups curried mayonnaise
salt and pepper to taste
8 slices cold chicken or 1 can
    cooked chicken

¼ cup French dressing
2 cups cold boiled rice
¾ cup orange chutney (or ¼ cup
    orange marmalade stirred
    into ½ cup chutney)

Soften gelatine in water, stir it into heated orange juice until it is dissolved. Cool and add to mayonnaise, season to taste and coat chicken slices with mayonnaise. Mix dressing with rice, mound on platter. Surround with chicken slices and garnish with piped mayonnaise and little mounds of chutney.

COLD BROILERS DORÉ

3 cups canned or cooked chicken,
    cut into large pieces
1 can hearts of palm, cut into 1-inch
    lengths
⅔ cup French dressing
¼ cup finely chopped onion
2 tablespoons chopped capers

1 hard-cooked egg, separated and
    riced
¼ cup chopped parsley
¼ cup chopped mushrooms
½ cup mayonnaise
1 head Boston lettuce

Line serving platter with lettuce leaves, arrange hearts of palm in center of platter and surround with chicken. Pour dressing over hearts of palm and top with onions, capers, egg and parsley. Whip mayonnaise and brush over chicken pieces, dust mayonnaise with mushrooms and serve.

CHICKEN CHASSEUR

1 roasted chicken, quartered
½ cup white wine
1 can button mushrooms
1 can drained tomatoes

1 can drained white onions
1 can chicken giblet gravy
salt and pepper
2 tablespoons chopped parsley

Heat all ingredients except parsley in a covered casserole in a moderately hot 375° F oven, to bubbling. Uncover, dust with parsley and serve.

ITALIAN CHICKEN HASH

1 can cream of chicken soup
1 tablespoon butter
2 tablespoons minced onion
2 tablespoons minced parsley

1 can chopped mushrooms, drained
salt and pepper
2 cups diced cold chicken
3 tablespoons sherry wine

Heat first 6 ingredients to boiling, add chicken and heat to boiling again. Add sherry, correct seasoning and serve.

ENGLISH CHICKEN HASH

1 can cream of chicken soup
1 tablespoon butter
1 tablespoon minced chives
2 tablespoons minced onion
1 can sliced potatoes, diced

2 cups diced cold chicken
salt and pepper
4 slices buttered toast
1 tablespoon minced chives
1 can cold figs

Heat first 7 ingredients to boiling, serve on buttered toast. Top with chives and accompany with iced figs.

CHAPTER 9.   *Vegetables*

I T may not be entirely fair to call them stepchildren, but the fact remains that our vegetables are often neglected and almost always prepared without thought or interest. They are usually just boiled and served as an accompaniment to fish or meat and rarely stand on their own feet as separate courses or even main dishes.

Vegetables are actually our latest and most valuable food asset. They are the only simple means at our disposal for weight reduction without harmful drugs, unnecessary expense or starvation—not to mention useless machinery and gymnasium equipment. Weight reduction is no longer a woman's fashion whim. It is more often a doctor's order—an order that can be followed with the utmost ease when there are enough vegetables on the menu.

Since there are countless canned vegetables available in the markets today, it is no longer necessary to lose hours each week to string, shell or peel them. Frozen vegetables may be prepared according to box directions and substituted for any of the canned vegetables suggested in these recipes. The NO COOKING vegetables are heated, but not in such a way that there is anything that can happen to them. They will not dry out, curdle or burn. All you have to do is heat and eat them.

ONIONS

2 cans small white onions, drained   salt and pepper
1 can apple juice   2 tablespoons minced parsley
½ bay leaf

Heat all ingredients in a buttered casserole in a moderate 350° F oven until onions are thoroughly heated through. Take out bay leaf and serve at once.

DUTCH ONIONS

2 cans white onions, drained   ¾ cup sour cream
1 can small peas, drained   2 tablespoons Parmesan
½ cup walnuts   salt and pepper
½ cup bread crumbs

Combine all ingredients in a buttered casserole and season to taste. Heat through in a moderately hot 375° F oven and serve.

SOUTHERN VEGETABLE CASSEROLE

1 can chicken gumbo soup   1 can small white onions
1 jar sliced okra   ½ garlic clove minced
2 tomatoes peeled, seeded and   salt and pepper
    diced   ¼ teaspoon basil, or to taste
2 hard-cooked eggs, sliced   ¼ teaspoon thyme, or to taste
1 can sliced mushrooms

Combine all ingredients in a buttered casserole. Season to taste and heat in a moderate 350° F oven. Serve at once.

WARSAW POTATOES

2 cans sliced potatoes   ½ cup sour cream
2 hard-cooked eggs, sliced   salt and pepper
½ jar herring in sour cream,
    chopped

Arrange potatoes and eggs in a buttered casserole, add herring and enough additional sour cream to coat generously. Cover and heat in a moderate oven 350° F until thoroughly heated through.

SOUR CREAM POTATOES

2 cans sliced potatoes	2 tablespoons chopped dill
2 chopped onions	salt and pepper to taste
¾ cup sour cream	½ cup grated horse radish

Combine first 5 ingredients in a buttered casserole, heat to boiling in a moderate oven 350° F and serve at once. Pass freshly grated horse radish on the side.

SWEET POTATOES

2 cans sweet potatoes	2 tablespoons brandy
1 can pineapple chunks	2 tablespoons butter
½ cup brown sugar	

Arrange sweet potatoes and pineapple chunks in a buttered casserole, add about ¼ cup pineapple juice, mix sugar, brandy and butter and spread over the top. Heat to bubbling in a moderate 350°F oven.

MOUSSE OF PEAS

1 envelope gelatine	3 cans peas
¼ cup cold consommé	¾ cup heavy cream, whipped
½ cup boiling consommé	salt, pepper and 1 pinch sugar
3 onion slices	a few drops green vegetable color

Empty gelatine into a cup, add cold consommé and set aside. Heat remaining consommé, pour over gelatine and stir until gelatine is dissolved. Blend peas and onion to a smooth purée, season and fold in cooled aspic and salted whipped cream. Add food coloring if desired, pour into rinsed ring mold and chill in coldest part of refrigerator for at least 2 hours. Unmold ring on a platter, fill with preferred tomato salad and serve with hot roast duck or chicken.

CARROTS

2 cans small whole carrots
¼ cup butter
salt and ½ teaspoon granulated
    sugar

½ cup milk
3 tablespoons chopped parsley
3 tablespoons chopped pecans

Heat carrots thoroughly in butter and milk with salt and sugar to taste. Dust with parsley and pecans and serve.

PEA PURÉE

(in electric blender)

3 cans peas
1 can purée of green pea soup
2 onion slices
¼ teaspoon green vegetable color

1 package fried onion rings,
    thawed
¼ cup heavy cream
salt, pepper and 1 pinch sugar

Blend peas with soup, cream, vegetable color, and raw onion into a smooth purée. Season and press into a buttered casserole, top with fried onion rings and heat thoroughly in a moderate 350° F oven.

COLD HERBED TOMATOES

1 teaspoon minced tarragon
1 teaspoon minced basil
1 teaspoon minced chives
1 lemon, juice and grated rind
1 tablespoon orange juice
1 teaspoon grated orange rind

salt and freshly ground black
    pepper
3 tablespoons tomato juice
4 tomatoes, peeled, sliced and
    chilled

Combine first 8 ingredients, shake well and chill for 2 hours. Pour over sliced tomatoes and serve.

FLAGEOLET BEANS

(These are lovely, tender little beans that look much like lima beans.)

2 cans flageolet beans
2 tablespoons minced parsley
1 cup apple cider
¼ cup chopped onion

¼ cup white raisins
salt and pepper
1 tablespoon salt butter

Heat beans to boiling with next 5 ingredients in their own liquor and cider. When beans are thoroughly heated, drain well, correct seasoning and stir in butter. Serve at once.

VEGETABLE CASSEROLE

1 can baby peas
1 can baby lima beans
1 bunch scallions, chopped
3 sprigs parsley

1 sprig thyme
1 can pearl corn
⅔ cup heavy cream, or to taste
salt and pepper

Combine all vegetables and herbs and bring to boil in their own liquor, season and drain well. Pour into buttered casserole, add cream to taste, correct seasoning and keep in 250° F oven until bubbling hot or until needed.

FRENCH TOMATOES

1 package frozen fried onion rings, thawed
1 tablespoon oil
1 large can tomatoes, well drained
½ cup cream
1 bay leaf

½ teaspoon dry tarragon
½ teaspoon dry thyme
roughly ground black pepper
salt
¼ cup chopped parsley

Chop onions, heat oil in casserole, add onions. Mix tomatoes, cream and seasonings and pour over onions. Heat to boiling and serve dusted with parsley.

SPINACH AND EGGS

2 cans spinach
1 can cream of spinach soup
4 5-minute eggs

salt and pepper
2 tablespoons minced ham

Combine spinach and soup, heat to boiling, season and press into hot casserole. Break egg shells, dip in cold water, peel carefully and lay on spinach. Top with ham and serve at once.

SPINACH SHERRY

2 cans spinach heated in its own
    liquid
½ cup garlic croutons

2 tablespoons sherry
salt and pepper
1 hard-cooked egg

Drain hot spinach well, add croutons and sherry. Season to taste, reheat and serve at once topped with riced egg.

GARLIC POTATOES

2 cans sliced potatoes
¼ cup grated cheese
salt and pepper
1 crushed garlic clove

2 tablespoons butter
1 cup milk
2 teaspoons grated orange rind

Drain potatoes well, combine with all ingredients and heat to boiling. Be sure potatoes are heated through before serving.

STUFFED BEETS

12 canned whole beets
1 3-ounce package cream cheese
2 tablespoons chopped gherkins or
    pickle relish
1 teaspoon capers

1 teaspoon chopped dill
1 teaspoon chopped chives
½ crushed garlic clove
salt and pepper
1 lemon or lime, cut into 4 wedges

Hollow out beets very carefully with a small melon scoop.

Fill with a mixture of the next 6 ingredients. Chill beets and serve with lemon or lime wedges with cold or hot meats.

POTATOES

2 cans white potatoes
2 tablespoons white wine
1 tablespoon oil

2 tablespoons chopped chives or
    parsley
1 tablespoon butter

Heat potatoes in their own liquor to boiling. Drain well and shake in a pan over low heat with all other ingredients until they are glossy and liquids are absorbed.

LYON POTATOES

2 cans sliced potatoes, drained
1 can onion soup

2 tablespoons minced chives
salt and pepper

Combine all ingredients, heat to boiling and serve. Reduce to ¾ can onion soup if desired.

HOT LIMA BEANS

1 cup bouillon
2 cans baby lima beans
2 tomatoes, peeled, sliced

4 frankfurters, sliced
salt, pepper
1 garlic clove

Bring bouillon to a boil, add remaining ingredients and stir well. Leave on stove at boiling point until vegetables and frankfurters are heated through. Stir well, correct seasoning and serve.

FRENCH BEANS

2 cans French-cut string beans
1 crushed garlic clove
2 tablespoons chopped basil or 1
    tablespoon dry

2 tablespoons soft butter
salt and pepper

Heat beans thoroughly in their own liquid with garlic. When they are heated through drain off liquid, add butter and shake well with chopped or dry basil, season and serve.

COLD BABY LIMA BEANS
(Good with steaks or chops)

2 cans baby lima beans	2 tablespoons chopped parsley
2 teaspoons prepared mustard	freshly ground black pepper
3 teaspoons paprika	2 tablespoons tarragon vinegar
1 clove garlic, crushed	¼ cup oil, or to taste
1 teaspoon salt	

Marinate well-drained beans in a dressing made of the remaining ingredients. Chill and serve with hot broiled meats.

YEAR-ROUND BEETS

2 jars whole baby beets	¼ cup bouillon
1 white onion, sliced thin and divided into rings	¼ teaspoon roughly ground black pepper
3 tablespoons sugar	¼ teaspoon salt or to taste
¼ cup tarragon vinegar	

Heat beets in their own juice, drain well, combine with last 5 ingredients, top with onion rings and heat again to boiling. Serve at once.

TURKISH BEETS

2 jars sliced beets	1 pinch nutmeg
1 tablespoon chopped chives	¼ pinch pepper
2 containers yoghurt	salt to taste
½ teaspoon cinnamon	

Heat beets to boiling in their own juice, beat chives, seasonings and spices into yoghurt. When beets are heated through, drain them well, add yoghurt and heat again. Serve hot.

POTATOES TIEPOLO

2 cans new potatoes
1 can tomatoes, well drained
salt and pepper

2 tablespoons chopped chives
½ cup garlic croutons

Heat potatoes and tomatoes to boiling. Add chives and season well. Heat croutons on a pan in a 250° F oven for a few minutes. Top with heated croutons and serve.

COLD ONIONS TARTAR
(Marvelous with hot meats or fish!)

2 cans small white onions, drained
¼ cup chopped parsley
¼ cup chopped stuffed olives

freshly ground black pepper
½ cup French Dressing # 2

Arrange onions in serving dish, pour over all other ingredients and chill before serving.

CREAMED ONIONS AND POTATOES

2 cans small white onions
1 can small white potatoes
1 can cream of mushroom soup

salt and pepper
3 tablespoons grated cheese
¼ cup chopped ham

Combine all ingredients, heat to boiling and serve.

CREAMED ONIONS

2 cans small white onions
1 can cream of onion soup
½ cup chopped walnuts

salt and pepper
¼ cup grated cheese

Combine all ingredients, season to taste, heat to boiling and serve.

ONIONS MIMOSA

2 cans small white onions
¼ cup white wine
¼ cup cream

¼ cup chopped parsley
1 hard-cooked egg, riced

Heat onions in their own liquor to boiling. Drain and reheat to boiling in wine and cream. Add parsley and serve with topping of egg.

HOT BABY PEAS

2 cans baby peas, drained
2 sprigs mint, chopped
4 tablespoons butter
2 teaspoons sugar

2 tablespoons heavy cream
salt and pepper
2 pieces buttered toast, cut into
    triangles

Combine first 6 ingredients, and heat thoroughly, stirring or shaking until peas are hot. Serve at once surrounded with toast triangles.

RICE AND MUSHROOMS

2 cans wild rice
2 cans button mushrooms
1 pinch cinnamon

salt and pepper
2 tablespoons minced parsley
2 tablespoons butter

Heat first 5 ingredients to boiling in liquor from mushroom cans. Stir well, add butter and shake until it is absorbed. Serve at once.

RICE AND PEAS

1 can wild rice
2 cans baby peas
2 tablespoons chopped parsley

1 tablespoon chopped chives
salt and pepper
2 tablespoons butter

Heat first 4 ingredients to boiling in the liquor from the peas. Drain well, season and shake with butter until butter is absorbed. Serve at once.

TOMATOES AND OKRA

1 large can tomatoes
½ teaspoon basil
½ teaspoon oregano
salt and pepper

1 can okra, drained
½ cup brown bread crumbs
½ cup grated cheese
¼ cup melted butter

Heat first 5 ingredients to boiling. Top with cheese mixed with crumbs. Pour heated butter over and serve.

TOMATOES AND RICE

½ garlic clove, crushed
2 tablespoons soft salt butter
4 tomatoes, peeled and sliced
1 can wild rice

¼ cup chopped onion
salt and pepper
½ cup bouillon

Mix garlic and butter, and set aside. Heat all other ingredients to boiling, drain well. Stir in garlic butter and serve at once.

PARSLEY POTATOES

2 cans small white potatoes
2 tablespoons butter
⅔ cup chopped parsley

salt and pepper
¼ teaspoon grated lemon rind
¼ teaspoon sugar

Heat potatoes as directed on can, drain well, shake in a pan with all other ingredients until they are coated. Season well and serve at once.

HOT KENT BEETS

2 cans tiny whole beets
4 cloves
1 tablespoon tarragon vinegar
½ tablespoon sugar
2 tablespoons butter

½ cup sour cream
1 teaspoon minced tarragon
1 teaspoon minced oregano
salt and pepper

Heat beets in their own juice with cloves, vinegar, sugar and butter. Take from fire, stir in sour cream, tarragon and oregano and season to taste. Serve at once.

RAITA

2 cups yoghurt
½ teaspoon powdered cummin
    seed
1 pinch chili powder
1 pinch powdered cardamon

¼ teaspoon each powdered cloves
    and cinnamon
salt to taste
4 tomatoes, peeled, seeded and
    sliced

1 cucumber, sliced paper thin

Beat yoghurt with ½ the spices until smooth. Pour over tomatoes and cucumber. Sprinkle with remaining spices and chill.

HOT BEETS I

2 cans beets with ½ their juice
¼ teaspoon ground cloves
2 teaspoons tarragon vinegar

2 teaspoons chopped dill
2 teaspoons sugar
salt and pepper to taste

Combine all ingredients, heat, stir and serve.

HOT BEETS II

2 cans beets with ½ their juice
3 tablespoons chopped shallots
2 teaspoons chopped dill

½ cup sour cream
salt and pepper to taste

Heat beets with shallots and dill, stir in sour cream and serve immediately.

CHAPTER 10.   *Relishes*

A RELISH is something taken with food to render it more enjoyable, and at the same time it is the quality with which food is
enjoyed. Just what that something is which can add even greater
pleasure to our meals is not firmly established. Judging by the relish
trays of some of our country inns it can be anything from a sweet
jelly to a carrot stick, from cottage cheese through all the gherkins
and pickles to the various chutneys. What most relishes do have in
common is a long cooking period and so they fall quite naturally
into the group of foods that enjoy their long cooking period in a
model plant and come to the table in a pretty jar or bottle. The
homemade relish has become rarer and scarcer, with the result that
there is now a faint resemblance in all relish trays. Here are a few
uncooked relishes that will break the monotony and add a pleasant
change. They can be made without effort and they will add relish
to any main course, which can then be enjoyed with relish and gusto.

SLICED DILL PICKLES

4 large dill pickles
2 cups granulated sugar
2 minced garlic cloves
1 teaspoon allspice

2 bay leaves
1 teaspoon mustard seed
1 teaspoon dill seed

Cut pickles across in thin slices, combine with their juices and all ingredients in a crock, cover and set aside in kitchen for 1 day. Chill and serve.

BEET RELISH

2 cans chopped beets, drained
1 cup chopped onion
1 jar red cabbage, drained
2 tablespoons well-drained horse radish

1 cup sugar
1 tablespoon salt
1 cup vinegar
½ teaspoon ground cloves

Bring all ingredients to boiling. Cool and chill.

SPICED CRANBERRY RELISH

1 can whole cranberry sauce
½ teaspoon cinnamon
½ teaspoon ground cloves

1 pinch salt
3 tablespoons minced orange rind
1 tablespoon minced lemon rind

Beat all other ingredients into the jelly, which has stood in kitchen for 1 hour. Chill for 2 hours and serve.

RAISIN RELISH

1 cup chili sauce
¾ cup red or white wine
¼ cup orange juice

¼ cup finely chopped onion
1 cup white raisins
salt and pepper

Heat chili sauce, wine, orange juice and onion to boiling. Pour over raisins, season to taste and set aside for 2 hours so that raisins will puff.

MAHARAJAH PEACHES

1 can peach halves
½ cup chutney, chopped

juice and grated rind of ½ lemon
1 tablespoon chopped mint

Heat peaches in their juice with all other ingredients and serve warm with meat or poultry.

MINTED CHUTNEY

1 cup roughly chopped mint leaves
1 chopped onion
1 peeled and cored apple, chopped

¼ cup sugar
1 tablespoon apricot jam
salt and pepper

Mince and then pound all the chopped ingredients into a paste, add sugar and jam, season to taste and serve with roast lamb.

ALMOND-STUFFED OLIVES

1 can pitted black olives
2 cloves garlic, crushed
1 teaspoon dry dill or 3 sprigs fresh dill

5 tablespoons grated onion and juice
1 can blanched almonds

Drain liquid from olives and add next 3 ingredients to it. Stuff olives with almonds, return to liquid and set in refrigerator for at least 3 days before serving.

PICKLED MUSHROOMS

3 pounds mushrooms, sliced
1 tablespoon mixed pickle spices
3 crushed garlic cloves
2 teaspoons salt or to taste
½ teaspoon pepper

½ cup vinegar
1 cup oil
1 teaspoon grated lemon rind
1 onion, chopped

Combine all ingredients in a bowl, cover and set aside in kitchen, stirring every hour, for 3 hours. Chill, pack in a jar and store in refrigerator. Serve with fish or meat. Add to antipasto or hors d'oeuvres tray.

PEPPER RELISH

1 cup chopped green pepper	3 tablespoons chopped parsley
1 cup chopped sweet red pepper	3 tablespoons chopped chives
1 chopped onion	¾ cup French Dressing # 3

Combine all ingredients, heat dressing to a boil, pour over peppers. Cool and chill for 3 hours.

RAW CRANBERRY RELISH

1 pound washed and picked cranberries	1 orange
	2 cups sugar

Cut outside rind from orange with potato parer. Cut orange in half, take out sections with a spoon, free of all white membranes and pits. Dice rind very finely. Put cranberries through food chopper, add orange meat and rind, add sugar, stir well and chill until needed.

CHAPTER 11.

Salads
and
Salad Dressings

Since most salads are, in any case, combinations of uncooked ingredients which are mixed and served, the following recipes try to suggest new combinations rather than repeating old ones. A few classic salads are included, but all formally arranged, draped and molded salads are omitted.

The salad course, which appears at various locations on the dinner menu, depending on geography, is another course that has barely had its surface scratched. There are salads to start the meal, there are salads that are the meal and there are salads to end the meal, and there are those that should be served after the meat and before the desserts.

There are salads also that should be served with meat and fish courses in place of hot vegetables, and salads that should be made especially for Sunday night suppers. These can be accompanied by only cheese and fruit and can make their evening the favorite of the week.

All the salads are easy to prepare and, as in other chapters, there is a little preparation necessary but NO COOKING.

KIDNEY BEAN SALAD

1 1-pound can red kidney beans
½ cup tarragon vinegar
¼ teaspoon freshly ground black pepper
3 tablespoons oil
¼ teaspoon dry mustard

½ teaspoon salt, or to taste
½ teaspoon minced chervil
2 small onions, thinly sliced and divided into rings
3 tablespoons chopped parsley

Drain beans, cover with vinegar and marinate 6 hours. Add next 5 ingredients, arrange in a salad bowl and top with onion rings and parsley.

POTATO SALAD

2 cans white Irish sliced potatoes
¼ cup chopped green pepper
1 slice ham, diced
4 stuffed olives, sliced

2 scallions or ½ onion, chopped
½ cup French Dressing # 3
3 tablespoons mayonnaise
lettuce leaves

Marinate potatoes in French dressing for an hour. Add pepper, ham, olives and scallions, bind with mayonnaise and serve in a lettuce-lined salad bowl.

Variations:
1. Add 1 smallest can lobster meat, omit ham.
2. Add 8 tablespoons smallest capers.
3. Omit ham and add same amount slivered bologna sausage.

PEARL CORN SALAD

2 1-pound cans white pearl corn
¼ cup minced onion
2 tablespoons chopped parsley
6 ripe pitted olives, chopped

⅔ cup French dressing
½ teaspoon paprika
3 tablespoons mayonnaise
2 peeled tomatoes

Combine first 4 ingredients, bind with dressing mixed with paprika and mayonnaise. Mound in a dish and surround with tomato slices.

CAESAR SALAD

1 head Boston lettuce	freshly ground black pepper
½ iceberg lettuce	juice and grated rind of 1 small
½ romaine lettuce	lemon
1 egg	½ cup grated Parmesan
1 teaspoon salt	½ cup crumbled Blue cheese
½ teaspoon dry mustard	1 cup garlic croutons (bottled)

Break all lettuces into salad bowl, break egg over greens, sprinkle with all other ingredients, and toss lightly until the egg is entirely absorbed.

PEARS WITH CHEESE

4 pears, halved and cored	salt and pepper
1 3-ounce package cream cheese	½ cup French Dressing # 2
3 tablespoons Blue cheese	lettuce leaves
2 tablespoons cream	1 cup cherries or grapes

Mix cheeses with cream and season to taste. Fill cheese into pear hollows and serve on lettuce leaves, pour over dressing and top each pear with seeded grapes or pitted cherries.

EGYPTIAN SALAD

½ can artichoke hearts (in brine)	1 pimiento, chopped
2 cups cold cooked rice	½ cup cooked green peas
½ cup diced ham	6 lettuce leaves
½ cup sliced raw mushrooms	¾ cup French Dressing # 3

Drain artichoke hearts and mix them with the next 5 ingredients. Arrange lettuce leaves in a salad bowl, mound the salad in the center and pour French dressing over it. Mix just before serving.

VINAIGRETTE SALAD

1 can hearts of palm	2 tablespoons chopped capers
1 hard-cooked egg	3 tablespoons chopped parsley
¼ cup chopped onion	⅔ cup French dressing

Chop egg white and rice egg yolk. Cut hearts of palm into 2-inch lengths, arrange on lettuce leaves. Pour over dressing and top with all other ingredients, ricing the egg yolk over the salad last of all.

Variations: This salad can be made by substituting green asparagus, white asparagus, artichokes, or cauliflower for the hearts of palm.

POTATO AND PIMIENTO SALAD

1 1-pound can white potatoes
1 jar pimientos, diced
½ cup French dressing
salt and pepper to taste
¼ cup finely chopped parsley
6 gherkins, chopped

Slice potatoes, combine all other ingredients except gherkins and allow potatoes to absorb dressing for an hour before serving. Add more dressing if necessary and serve topped with gherkins.

PLAIN LETTUCE SALAD

3 Boston lettuces or assorted greens
3 sprigs chervil, chopped
3 spring onions, chopped
1½ tablespoons vinegar
½ teaspoon salt
¼ teaspoon pepper
¼ teaspoon dry mustard
2½ tablespoons olive oil

Dissolve salt and mustard in vinegar, add pepper and oil and shake or stir until smooth. Use the tender inside leaves and hearts of the lettuces, place in a salad bowl with chervil and spring onions and pour dressing over just before serving. Stir or "fatigue" only while serving.

EGG SALAD

8 hard-cooked eggs
4 sprigs chervil or 2 teaspoons dry chervil
1 bunch spring onions, chopped
8 lettuce leaves
½ cup mayonnaise
1 tablespoon vinegar
3 tablespoons oil
salt and pepper to taste

Quarter 6 of the hard-cooked eggs. Arrange on lettuce leaves on 4 plates. Pound 2 egg yolks with mayonnaise and beat in vinegar and oil, season sauce to taste, pour over the eggs and top with chervil and spring onion. Use 2 left-over egg whites on a dressing for a vegetable salad.

AÏDA SALAD

1 can artichoke hearts in brine
4 stalks Belgian endive, quartered
    lengthwise
1 small Boston lettuce
2 tomatoes, peeled and sliced

½ green pepper, seeded and diced
2 hard-cooked eggs, riced
1 teaspoon prepared mustard
½ cup French Dressing # 1

Drain artichokes and cut them in half lengthwise. Arrange endive and lettuce in salad bowl, add artichokes mixed with next 3 ingredients. Stir mustard into French dressing and pour over the salad. Mix just before serving.

STUFFED AVOCADOS OR ALLIGATOR PEARS

Avocados lend themselves well to stuffing as they present a perfect one-portion cavity when they are cut in half lengthwise and the stone is removed.

The filling may be prepared in advance, but the avocado should not be cut until the last moment as the edges wilt and the meat turns brown if they stand too long after being cut.

They may be filled with:

> French Dressing
> Roquefort Dressing
> Endive Salad
> Shrimp Salad
> Lobster Salad
> Grapefruit Sections with French Dressing
> Rum and Lime Juice, instead of dressing
> Rum and Powdered Ginger, instead of dressing
> Jellied Madrilene Soup

SPANISH SALAD

1 can sliced mushrooms or ¾ cup
    raw sliced mushrooms
¼ cup chopped green pepper
2 pimientos, diced
1½ cups cold cooked rice

½ cup French Dressing # 1
2 tablespoons chopped parsley
1 tablespoon lemon juice
½ head lettuce

Mix all ingredients with dressing and serve in a lettuce-lined salad bowl.

MIXED VEGETABLE SALAD

1 1-pound can mixed vegetables
¾ cup curry mayonnaise
1 small Boston lettuce head

½ cup small rosettes of raw
    cauliflower
salt and pepper to taste

Arrange lettuce leaves in salad bowl, mix vegetables and cauliflower with mayonnaise and mound in bowl.
Note: This can be made into a hearty salad by adding a can of salmon or tuna fish and arranging the fish around the vegetable salad.

RICE SALAD THEODORE
(for six)

4 medium cucumbers
1 teaspoon salt
3 cups cooked rice
¼ cup chopped chives
¼ cup chopped parsley

1 head Boston lettuce
3 large or 4 small tomatoes, peeled
    and sliced
1 medium onion sliced paper thin
    and separated into rings

Dressing:

1 teaspoon salt
1 teaspoon sugar
1 teaspoon dry yellow mustard
1 teaspoon paprika

⅓ cup tarragon vinegar
⅓ cup olive oil
⅓ cup vegetable oil

Score cucumbers with fork or fluted knife, cut into 6 strips lengthwise and cut away the seeds. Cut strips into 1-inch-long sections diagonally, place in a wide bowl and salt. Put a weighted saucer on top and set aside for ½ hour. Mix rice, chives and parsley and add the well-drained cucumbers. Arrange lettuce leaves in a salad bowl, mound the rice salad in the center, circle with overlapping tomato slices and lay thin onion rings on the tomatoes.

Prepare dressing and pour over the salad at serving time. Mix the salad and serve immediately.

FRANKFORT SALAD

4 frankfurters, skinned and cut across in thin slices
4 slices Swiss cheese, diced
2 hard-cooked eggs, riced

¼ cup chopped chives
1 dill pickle, chopped
½ head Boston lettuce

Dressing:

6 tablespoons mayonnaise
2 teaspoons prepared mustard
1 teaspoon Worcestershire sauce

1 teaspoon A—1 Sauce
salt and pepper to taste

Mix all ingredients with the dressing and serve in a salad bowl on lettuce leaves.

NIÇOISE

8 5-minute eggs, chilled and peeled
8 thick tomato slices
1 can French-cut string beans
5 tablespoons mayonnaise
2 cans green asparagus spears

8 truffle slices or ripe olive slices
1½ cups green mayonnaise (sauce verte)
salt and pepper to taste
1 radish

For an elaborate luncheon or buffet, line platter with aspic. See "Aspic Mirror."

Arrange eggs on tomato slices around a platter. Center with a mound of beans bound with mayonnaise and place asparagus spears on either side of beans. Place a truffle slice on each egg and pass a sauce bowl of green mayonnaise separately. Garnish with parsley and place a red radish rose in the center of the bean salad.

STUFFED APPLE SALAD

4 large green or red apples
½ cup diced celery
½ cup chopped nuts
½ cup mayonnaise or to taste

1 apple peeled, cored and diced
salt and pepper to taste
apple or lemon leaves

Cut tops from apples, carefully scoop out pulp and use for apple sauce. Fill the apples with a salad made of remaining ingredients and serve garnished with green leaves.

FRUIT SALAD

1½ cups fresh diced pineapple
1 cup peeled, diced apple
1 cup celery, diced
¾ cup mayonnaise

2 tablespoons sherry
1 tablespoon heavy cream
2 teaspoons tarragon vinegar
½ teaspoon paprika

Place fruit and celery in salad bowl on lettuce leaves. Mix remaining ingredients and pour over salad.

RUSSIAN SALAD

2 smoked herrings, diced
2 beets, chopped
2 hard-cooked eggs, separated and riced
2 tablespoons fresh ground horse radish

2 tablespoons olive oil
1 tablespoon tarragon vinegar
1 tablespoon parsley, chopped
⅛ teaspoon powdered cloves
fresh ground pepper
salt to taste

Mix and serve.

WATER CRESS AND AVOCADO SALAD

1 bunch water cress
1 avocado pear
½ cup garlic croutons (bottled)

½ cup French Dressing # 3
½ lemon, juice and grated rind

Wash and clean cress, wrap in foil and chill. Peel pear, sprinkle with lemon juice. Put cress in salad bowl, top with diced pear and croutons, pour dressing over and dust with lemon rind. Mix the salad just before serving, or arrange on individual plates and pass dressing separately.

SHRIMPS IN ALLIGATOR PEAR

2 large alligator pears cut in half
    lengthwise
1 lemon
1½ cups peeled, cooked shrimps
    cut in half
¾ cup mayonnaise
2 tablespoons minced parsley

2 tablespoons minced onion
salt and pepper
2 hard-cooked egg yolks
shredded lettuce
4 lemon wedges
4 parsley sprigs for garnish

Remove stones from pears, sprinkle with lemon juice, fill with shrimps mixed with mayonnaise, parsley and onion and seasoned to taste. Rice egg yolks over the pears, set on shredded lettuce and serve with lemon wedges and parsley sprigs.

PEAR SALAD

2 pears, peeled and sliced
1 bunch water cress
1 small head Boston lettuce
1 tablespoon chutney, chopped fine
½ teaspoon sugar

4 tablespoons oil
2 tablespoons vinegar
1 teaspoon salt
¼ teaspoon pepper

Arrange cleaned water cress and lettuce with the pears in a salad bowl. Combine all other ingredients and pour over the salad. Toss and serve.

TOMATO PECAN AND EGG SALAD

3 tomatoes, peeled, sliced
    horizontally and drained
2 sliced hard-cooked eggs
6 scallions cut crosswise into ¼
    inch slices

½ cup roughly chopped pecans
3 tablespoons chopped parsley
¼ cup French Dressing # 4

Arrange tomato and egg slices in bowl, top with scallions, pecans and parsley. Pour over dressing and mix just before serving.

COLE SLAW

1 head cabbage
1 tablespoon chopped parsley
1 tablespoon chopped chives
½ cup vinegar
1 tablespoon sugar

1 tablespoon prepared mustard
¼ cup cream
1 teaspoon celery salt
pepper to taste
paprika

Shred cabbage, mix with parsley and chives. Shake next 6 ingredients into a smooth dressing, pour over cabbage and dust with paprika.

CABBAGE SALAD

1 medium white cabbage, finely shredded
2 onions, sliced thin
4 cooking apples, peeled, cored and thinly sliced
¾ cup oil

¼ cup lemon juice
2 teaspoons salt, or to taste
⅓ cup sour cream
3 tablespoons chopped parsley, or chives
freshly ground black pepper

Mix cabbage, onions and apples, add a dressing made of the next 6 ingredients and stir well. Cover and set aside for 3 hours.

BEET SALAD

1 can sliced beets, drained and chilled
1 small onion, sliced thin and divided into rings

¼ cup French Dressing # 1
2 teaspoons fresh-grated or bottled horse radish
lettuce leaves

Arrange beets and onion on lettuce leaves. Mix horse radish with dressing, pour over and serve.

TOMATO SALAD

3 peeled tomatoes, sliced
    horizontally
1 thinly sliced cucumber
2 white onions, peeled, cut into
    paper-thin slices and divided
    into rings

½ cup French Dressing # 1
1 tablespoon minced parsley
1 teaspoon minced dill
1 teaspoon minced chervil
½ teaspoon rosemary

Chill, mix all ingredients and serve.

ENDIVE AND BEET SALAD

1 jar shoestring-cut beets, drained
4 stalks Belgian endive, cut across
    in ¼ inch slices

½ cup French Dressing # 2
1 teaspoon grated orange rind
1 hard-cooked egg, riced

Mix all ingredients and serve cold.

EGG AND ASPARAGUS SALAD

2 tablespoons finely chopped onion
2 tablespoons finely chopped
    capers
2 tablespoons chopped parsley
⅔ cup French Dressing # 1

4 5-minute eggs
1 1-pound can green asparagus
    spears
1 head Boston lettuce

Add first 3 ingredients to dressing, arrange eggs on asparagus
spears in lettuce-lined salad bowl, pour dressing over and serve.

SPINACH AND EGG SALAD

½ small head iceberg lettuce
2 cups spinach leaves loosely
    packed
3 hard-cooked eggs, sliced

6 radishes, sliced
1 tablespoon chopped chives
⅓–½ cup French Dressing # 4

Mix and serve.

CHIFFONADE SALAD I

½ pound Belgian endive cut
  lengthwise
½ head chicory or Boston lettuce
½ jar shoestring beets, drained

¼ cup Lemon French Dressing
  (see page 162)
1 tablespoon minced capers
1 hard-cooked egg, riced
2 tablespoons chopped parsley

Arrange spikes of endive on lettuce leaves, top with beets and capers and pour French dressing over them. Dust with riced egg and chopped parsley and serve.

CHIFFONADE II

½ head Boston lettuce
½ romaine
½ escarole
2 tomatoes, peeled, seeded and
  sliced

½ jar shoestring beets
2 stalks celery, strings removed and
  cut julienne

Dressing:

1 hard-cooked egg, riced
½ teaspoon paprika
½ teaspoon salt
¼ teaspoon pepper
½ teaspoon Dijon prepared
  mustard

2 teaspoons minced chives
1 teaspoon minced tarragon
6 tablespoons oil
3 tablespoons vinegar

Prepare greens, tomatoes, beets and celery in salad bowl. Crush the riced egg with the next 6 dressing ingredients, stir in oil and vinegar and pour over salad.

PEASANT SALAD

(A splendid Sunday night supper with garlic bread and red wine!)

1 can small white potatoes
8 slices bologna sausage
1 pound Swiss cheese
1 dill pickle, sliced
1 small onion, chopped

1 clove garlic, crushed
1 cup French Dressing # 1
salt and pepper to taste
2 peeled tomatoes, sliced
2 hard-cooked eggs, sliced

Rinse, dry and slice potatoes. Cut bologna and cheese into discs with smallest cookie cutter and combine with potatoes, pickle and onion. Add garlic to French dressing and pour over salad. Cover and set aside for 1 hour. Mound salad in a bowl and surround with alternating slices of peeled tomatoes and hard-cooked eggs.

SALADE BONNE FEMME

1 pound Swiss cheese, slivered
1 can small white potatoes
1 celery heart with inside stalks and yellow leaves, chopped
¼ cup chopped onion
⅔ cup mayonnaise

2 teaspoons prepared mustard
½ teaspoon Worcestershire sauce
salt and freshly ground black pepper to taste
1 head Boston lettuce
½ cup chopped walnuts

Rinse, dry and slice potatoes finely and mix with cheese, celery and onion. Add mustard and Worcestershire to mayonnaise and season to taste. Bind the salad with the mayonnaise, mound it on lettuce leaves in a salad bowl and dust with walnuts.

SALADE AU FROMAGE

⅓ cup oil
2 tablespoons vinegar
2 tablespoons cream
½ teaspoon salt
¼ teaspoon pepper
1 teaspoon minced onion

1 teaspoon prepared mustard
3 slices Swiss cheese
½ head iceberg lettuce
1 head Boston lettuce
1 head romaine
1 tablespoon chopped chives

Make a dressing of first 7 ingredients. Dice the cheese, or if a very small cutter is available, cut the cheese into dime-sized discs. Add cheese to dressing and pour it over a bowl of prepared salad greens. Toss well and serve either as a salad or as a dessert with crisp bread and cold grapes.

BRUSSELS SALAD

6 heads Belgian endive
6 ounces Gruyère cheese
1 tablespoon prepared mustard
juice and grated rind of 1 lemon

3 tablespoons mayonnaise
¼ cup whipped cream
1 head Boston lettuce

Cut endive into quarters lengthwise and cut cheese into strips the same length as the endive. Arrange cheese and endive neatly, as if stacking logs, on lettuce leaves on 4 salad plates. Mix mustard and lemon juice with mayonnaise and fold in whipped cream. Pour dressing over the endive and cheese and dust with grated lemon rind.

FILLED TOMATOES

½ cup Blue cheese
1 8-ounce package cream cheese
¼ cup butter
2 hard-cooked egg yolks
2 teaspoons paprika

salt to taste
4 large tomatoes, peeled
1 can flat anchovy fillets
1 head Boston lettuce

Work first 6 ingredients into a smooth paste. Cut tomatoes in half crosswise, drain for 15 minutes and dry the cut surface. Pipe the cheese mixture onto the tomatoes and cover with a lattice of anchovy fillets, cut in half lengthwise. Serve on lettuce leaves in a shallow salad bowl.

CHEESE, TOMATO AND RADISH SALAD

1 bunch radishes, chopped
2 tablespoons mayonnaise
salt and freshly ground black
    pepper to taste
1 head Boston lettuce

4 peeled tomatoes, halved
2 slices Swiss cheese, diced
1 small onion, chopped
¼ cup French Dressing # 1
¼ cup chopped chives

Bind radishes with mayonnaise and season to taste. Line salad bowl with lettuce leaves and mound radish salad in center. Surround with tomato halves covered with mixture of cheese and onion. Pour French Dressing # 1 over the tomatoes and dust with chives.

CURAÇAO SALAD

1 can pineapple chunks
2 sliced peaches
1 cup hulled strawberries

½ cup French dressing
2 tablespoons curaçao
¼ cup whipped cream

Combine fruits, mix dressing with curaçao and whipped cream and pour over fruit.

BASIC FRENCH DRESSING #1

1 teaspoon salt
½ teaspoon pepper
4 tablespoons lemon juice or
    vinegar

½ garlic clove, optional
1 teaspoon prepared mustard,
    optional
1 cup oil

Shake or beat all ingredients. Take out garlic clove and serve. If dressing is to be stored, let garlic remain in dressing. Add 1 tablespoon honey if dressing is intended for fruit salads.

BASIC FRENCH DRESSING #2

⅓ cup tarragon vinegar
1 teaspoon salt
¼ teaspoon black pepper
1 teaspoon paprika

1 teaspoon dry mustard
2 teaspoons sugar
1 cup oil

Stir dry ingredients with vinegar until salt and sugar are dissolved. Add oil gradually, stirring until the dressing is smooth and slightly thickened. Dressing may also be mixed by placing all ingredients in electric blender and blending for ½ minute.

BASIC FRENCH DRESSING #3

½ teaspoon salt
½ teaspoon dry mustard
¼ teaspoon dry basil
1 pinch celery seed

3 tablespoons tarragon vinegar
¼ cup olive oil
¼ cup vegetable oil
1 teaspoon minced onion

Crush salt, mustard, basil and celery seed with a wooden spoon in a small bowl, add all other ingredients and beat with a rotary beater, or place all ingredients in a blender and blend for ½ minute until thick and creamy.

BASIC MAYONNAISE #1

2 egg yolks
½ teaspoon salt
¼ teaspoon dry mustard powder
1 pinch white pepper

2 teaspoons tarragon vinegar
1 teaspoon lemon juice
1 cup oil

Stir egg yolks until they are smooth with a fork or wire whisk or beat them with a rotary hand beater or an electric beater. Add salt, dry mustard, pepper and 1 teaspoon vinegar and stir or beat until smooth. Gradually add ¼ cup oil, drop by drop, while stirring or beating constantly. Add the remaining vinegar and stir or beat in ¼ cup oil, drop by drop, as before. Add lemon juice and stir or beat in remaining oil, in a thin stream, making sure the oil is being absorbed as it is stirred in. Scrape the sides of the bowl several times and continue to stir or beat constantly until the sauce is smooth.

All vinegar or all lemon juice can be substituted for the vinegar and lemon juice combination.

Lemon Mayonnaise Variation:

Prepare mayonnaise as above, using all lemon juice instead of vinegar and lemon juice and add the grated rind of 1 lemon to the sauce. Serve with cold trout or salmon.

BASIC MAYONNAISE #2

(in electric blender)

1 tablespoon lemon juice
1 tablespoon vinegar
½ teaspoon salt
¼ teaspoon dry basil

¼ teaspoon dry mustard
1 egg
½ cup olive oil
½ cup vegetable oil

Blend first 5 ingredients for 3 seconds, add egg, blend 1 second, add 2 tablespoons oil and blend again for 3 seconds. Continue to blend, adding rest of oil slowly in a thin stream until mayonnaise is thick and oil is used up.

Lemon Mayonnaise Variation:

Substitute 2 tablespoons lemon juice for lemon juice and vinegar in Basic Mayonnaise # 2, omit the basil and add the thinly cut yellow peel of one lemon. Blend after the peel is added until it is very fine.

BASIC MAYONNAISE #3

½ teaspoon prepared mustard
½ teaspoon sugar
½ teaspoon salt
1 pinch cayenne and white pepper
3 egg yolks

1 tablespoon tarragon vinegar
1 cup oil
2 tablespoons lemon juice
⅓ cup cream, half whipped

Mix dry ingredients with yolks and vinegar. Beat in oil, drop by drop, add lemon juice gradually after half the oil is incorporated. Add rest of oil a little more quickly, beating or stirring constantly. Add cream and serve with fruit salads.

RED CURRANT DRESSING

½ teaspoon English mustard
1 cup French dressing

¼ cup melted currant jelly

Dissolve mustard in dressing, add jelly, shake well and serve well chilled with fruit salads.

BLUE CHEESE DRESSING

¼ cup Blue cheese, crumbled
½ teaspoon salt
½ teaspoon paprika
½ teaspoon dry mustard

dash black pepper
dash cayenne
½ cup oil
¼ cup vinegar

Combine all ingredients in a jar or shaker, cover and shake well. Pour over green salad and toss. Also good on tomato or endive salad. Makes about 1 cup.

DILL DRESSING

¼ teaspoon black pepper
½ teaspoon salt
2 tablespoons tarragon vinegar
4 tablespoons oil

2 teaspoons dried dill, or fresh chopped dill
1 hard-cooked egg white, chopped fine

Mix and serve over Boston lettuce or cucumber salad.

RICHARD'S DRESSING
(Use the back of your wooden salad spoon to crush all this together in the salad bowl.)

1 teaspoon coarse salt
½ teaspoon freshly ground coarse black pepper
½ teaspoon dry English mustard

1 teaspoon oregano
¼ clove garlic, crushed
3 tablespoons oil
2 tablespoons vinegar

Add crisp salad greens, toss and serve.

MINT DRESSING

1 cup oil
⅓ cup vinegar
1 teaspoon salt

¼ teaspoon pepper
1½ tablespoons chopped mint
½ tablespoon chopped onion

Mix all ingredients and chill. Shake before serving. Yield: approximately 1⅓ cups.

LEMON FRENCH DRESSING

½ teaspoon salt
¼ teaspoon freshly ground black pepper
1½ tablespoons tarragon vinegar

1½ tablespoons lemon juice
6 tablespoons salad oil
1 teaspoon minced parsley

Stir salt and pepper into vinegar and lemon juice, stir in oil and add parsley last of all, or shake all ingredients in a bottle until salt is dissolved and dressing is smooth.

MUSTARD DRESSING

1 teaspoon mustard powder
1 tablespoon prepared mustard
¼ cup vinegar
¼ cup heavy cream

¼ cup oil
½ teaspoon salt
1 pinch cayenne
½ crushed garlic clove

Shake all ingredients in a jar, correct seasoning and serve.

WHITE FLOWER FARM DRESSING

½ teaspoon roughly ground black
    pepper
½ teaspoon dry mustard
¼ teaspoon anise seed
1 tablespoon rough salt

4 tablespoons oil
1 tablespoon vinegar
4 dashes Maggi seasoning
1 clove garlic

Rub wooden salad bowl with garlic. Crush all dry ingredients together in bottom of bowl with wooden spoon. Stir in oil and vinegar, add greens, toss well and serve.

CHAPTER 12.   *Sauces*

H ERE are sauces to serve with fish, meat, eggs, vegetables and desserts and all of them are, as promised, prepared without cooking.
Some have to be heated, some have to be chilled, in a few cases a cup
of jelly has to be melted over hot water, but none of them can possi-
bly *separate*—that greatest disaster of sauce-making!

If the hostess or housewife is an experienced cook, she can look
here for sauces that will take less time and show more originality.
If she is inexperienced, she can forget the Roux, the Espagnoles and
the Béchamels that cause her so much concern, and find sauces that
require no skill to prepare and serve them with any course.

Few people have time today to clarify stock and reduce liquids.
When they have enough leisure to make a beautiful, traditional
sauce for the main course they rarely have time over for anything
else. They will be all the better off if they can find a dessert sauce
and a dressing that can be made in seconds.

Some of the following sauces are old and famous, some are new
and original but all of them have one thing in common, they only
have to be mixed before they are served.

AÏOLI
(Needless to say, this sauce should only be served to 4 people who really like garlic!)

8 cloves garlic, crushed
½ teaspoon salt
1 ice cube

2 egg yolks
1⅓ cups olive oil
1 teaspoon lemon juice

Crush garlic and salt into a paste, add ice cube and egg yolks and stir once, discard the ice. Add oil, drop by drop, stirring constantly as for mayonnaise. Add lemon juice, correct seasoning and thin with a few drops of water if necessary. Serve with meat or fish.

Reduce garlic to 4 cloves if you want to walk among your fellow men.

BASIC COCKTAIL SAUCE
(For Clam and Oyster and All Sea Food Cocktails)

1 bottle chili sauce
¼ cup lemon juice
2 tablespoons horse radish, drained
1 tablespoon Worcestershire sauce

1 tablespoon grated onion
½ teaspoon salt
1 dash Tabasco Sauce

Serve plain or add mayonnaise to taste.

SHRIMP, LOBSTER OR CRABMEAT COCKTAIL SAUCE

¾ cup mayonnaise
¼ cup chili sauce
1 tablespoon prepared mustard
½ teaspoon onion juice

2 tablespoons well-drained sweet
pickle relish
2 teaspoons capers
½ teaspoon salt

½ teaspoon pepper

Mix all ingredients and serve cold with any sea food cocktail.

SAUCE PRINCE De GALLES

2 hard-cooked egg yolks, riced
¼ cup vinegar
½ cup oil
1 teaspoon Dijon mustard
1 pinch saffron, optional
⅔ cup mayonnaise

½ cup minced herbs, parsley,
  chives, spinach leaves,
  chervil and tarragon, or any
  combination
1 pinch cayenne
salt and pepper to taste

Stir the riced egg yolks with vinegar and oil until they are smooth. Add mustard and saffron powder and gradually stir in the mayonnaise and minced herbs. Season to taste and serve chilled with cold meats, poultry, fish or vegetables.

CHERRY SAUCE

1 can tart, pitted cherries
½ cup brown sugar
½ cup currant jelly

¼ teaspoon ground cloves
¼ teaspoon cinnamon
grated rind and juice of ½ lemon

Heat currant jelly over hot water until it is melted, add drained cherries and all other ingredients. Thin sauce to taste with cherry juice. Stir well and serve hot with ham. To serve cold: add sugar, cloves and cinnamon to hot currant jelly, stir well, take from heat and add cherries, lemon juice and rind. Thin with cherry juice and chill. Serve with ham or any roast meat.

SAUCE VERT-PRÉ

1 cup mayonnaise
3 tablespoons chopped dill pickle
2 tablespoons creamed butter
2 tablespoons chopped shallots
2 tablespoons chopped parsley
2 tablespoons chopped capers

1 tablespoon anchovy paste
1 tablespoon chopped chervil
1 tablespoon chopped tarragon
salt and pepper to taste
1 cup whipped cream

Stir next 8 ingredients into the mayonnaise, add salt and pepper to taste and fold in the whipped cream. Serve with all fried foods, especially shrimp or corn fritters, although it does very nicely with breaded fried mushrooms too.

DILL MUSTARD SAUCE

½ cup brown mustard
3 tablespoons mayonnaise
2 tablespoons sour cream
2 tablespoons vinegar
1 tablespoon sugar

2 tablespoons chopped dill
1 squeeze lemon juice
½ teaspoon black pepper
½ teaspoon salt, or to taste

Stir all ingredients together or blend them in an electric blender. Serve with any fish, but it's especially good with fillets of herring.

SAUCE VINAIGRETTE

2 tablespoons chopped shallots
1 tablespoon chopped onion
1 tablespoon chopped capers
2 teaspoons chopped dill

2 teaspoons chopped tarragon
1 cup French Dressing # 3
1 hard-cooked egg, riced

Thoroughly stir first 5 ingredients into the dressing and add the riced hard-cooked egg. For salads and cold vegetables. Very good with asparagus, hearts of palm, artichoke and cauliflower.

GROUND VEGETABLE CREAM SAUCE

½ cup oil
2 egg yolks
¾ container yoghurt
1 teaspoon lemon juice

salt and pepper to taste
½ cup ground cucumber, celery or
    cauliflower

Stir oil into yolks drop by drop, gradually add other ingredients and increase yoghurt if sauce is too thick. Serve with hot or cold chicken or pour over potato salad, using approximately 2 pounds potatoes. This may be used as a meat or salad sauce. Left-over ground cooked vegetables may be substituted for the raw vegetables.

Serve this cream sauce over 1½ pounds peeled and sliced tomatoes, top with chives or spring onions.

ALMOND PAPRIKA SAUCE

Make sauce as ground vegetable cream sauce, but substitute 2 ounces scalded and ground almonds and ½ cup seeded minced green pepper for the ground vegetables.

Serve with boiled potatoes, boiled cauliflower or pour it over a potato salad.

SAUCE DES HALLES

3 shallots, minced
3 tablespoons red wine vinegar

1 tablespoon roughly ground black pepper (preferably Tellicherry pepper)

Mix and serve with oysters.

GENOESE SAUCE

4 garlic cloves
3 sprigs each fresh sweet basil and marjoram
½ teaspoon salt

¾ cup grated Parmesan cheese
½ cup oil
3 tablespoons ground walnuts
¼ cup boiling consommé or water

Crush garlic with herbs and salt. Stir in Parmesan and gradually add oil, drop by drop as in making mayonnaise (see page 160). Add walnuts and thin to desired consistency with consommé or water. Serve with Italian pasta.

INDIAN MAYONNAISE

1 clove garlic, crushed
2 teaspoons curry powder

½ cup mayonnaise, or more to taste

Crush garlic with curry powder and stir in mayonnaise to taste. Serve with fried fish or cold boiled salmon.

SAUCE MOUSQUETAIRE

2 tablespoons butter
1 cup mayonnaise
3 drops Maggi seasoning
3 tablespoons minched shallots

1 tablespoon chopped chives
1 tablespoon chopped tarragon
salt, pepper and cayenne to taste

Cream butter, whip it into mayonnaise with Maggi seasoning. add shallots, herbs and seasoning and chill before serving. Serve with beef or fish.

RED WINE SAUCE

1 cup red wine
1 cup consommé
½ cup brandy

½ cup dark brown sugar
½ cup tomato catsup
salt and pepper to taste

Heat all ingredients over hot water. Stir until sugar is melted and serve with meat or poultry.

SWEDISH SAUCE

1 cup mayonnaise
¼ cup tart apple sauce

1 tablespoon grated horse radish
salt and pepper to taste

Mix all ingredients, chill and serve with cold meat.

CUMBERLAND SAUCE

1 cup currant jelly
¼ cup Madeira
¼ cup slivered orange rind
1 tablespoon slivered lemon rind

1 small piece ginger chopped or
      powdered ginger to taste
½ teaspoon dry mustard
1 pinch cayenne

Melt currant jelly over hot water, add all other ingredients and serve warm or cold with hot or cold meats, or pour it over a bowl of fresh strawberries and serve the strawberries with a hot ham.

CONTINENTAL CUMBERLAND SAUCE

1 cup red wine
1 sliced shallot
1 orange rind, slivered
½ teaspoon ground cloves
2 teaspoons English mustard

2 teaspoons horse radish powder
1 pinch sugar
1 jar lingonberries
juice of 1 orange

Peel orange with potato peeler to obtain the outside rind only. Heat red wine with next 6 ingredients. Blend with lingonberries and add orange juice to taste. Serve with game of any kind.

CUCUMBER SAUCE

½ cup mayonnaise
½ cup sour cream
1 unpeeled cucumber, finely
    chopped
1 onion, finely chopped

2 tablespoons lemon juice
¼ teaspoon celery salt
¼ cup finely chopped salted
    almonds or filberts

Combine first 6 ingredients. Add nuts and serve chilled with roast chicken or cold fish. The nicest way to serve it is with a sizzling-hot young broiler, a fat one.

MUSTARD SAUCE

2 tablespoons chopped tarragon
¼ cup brown or French mustard
1 cup mayonnaise

½ teaspoon salt, or to taste
¼ teaspoon pepper

Mix or blend all ingredients and serve with fish or meat. It's an easy sauce to make and serves a lot of purposes.

FROZEN SWEDISH CREAM

½ cup cream, whipped
2 tablespoons finely grated fresh
    horse radish

2 teaspoons mayonnaise
1 teaspoon French mustard
salt to taste

Fold all ingredients into whipped cream, pipe into rosettes and freeze on waxed paper. Place on hot meat, game or fish at the moment of serving.

SAUCE TARTARE #1

To 1 cup of Basic Mayonnaise add:

2 tablespoons chopped onion
2 tablespoons chopped gherkins
2 tablespoons chopped capers
½ tablespoon finely minced
    parsley

1 teaspoon chopped chives, chervil
    or tarragon or any preferred
    herb

Mix all above ingredients and serve with breaded and fried foods. Good with fried scallops, crabs, oysters and all sea food.

SAUCE TARTARE #2

1 cup mayonnaise
2 tablespoons chopped capers
2 tablespoons chopped onion
2 tablespoons pickle relish

1 tablespoon chopped chives
1 teaspoon prepared mustard
salt and pepper to taste

Mix all ingredients and serve with fried or breaded fish or meat, fried mushrooms or fritters.

SAUCE DUMAS

1 can tuna fish
6 tablespoons oil
3 tablespoons vinegar
1 teaspoon anchovy paste

1 teaspoon mustard
1 hard-cooked egg, riced
2 tablespoons chopped dill pickle
1 tablespoon capers

Mash and stir tuna fish with oil and vinegar until smooth. Mix with all other ingredients and serve cold with fish or cold veal.

HERBED MAYONNAISE FOR FISH
OR COCKTAILS

(in electric blender)

1 cup mayonnaise
½ cup sour cream
1 tablespoon dry chives
1 teaspoon capers
1 teaspoon tarragon

½ teaspoon dry dill
1 clove garlic, crushed
4 sprigs parsley
salt and pepper to taste

Blend all ingredients ½ minute, chill and serve. Use fresh herbs if they can be obtained.

SAUCE POLONAISE

¼ cup butter
2 tablespoons sugar
1 tablespoon mustard

½ cup orange juice
¼ cup lemon juice
1 pinch of salt

Cream butter with sugar, stir in mustard, salt and fruit juices until a smooth sauce is obtained. Serve with fish.

SAUCE RAIFORT
(Horse Radish Sauce)

½ cup grated horse radish
¼ cup tarragon vinegar
¼ cup orange juice

1 teaspoon sugar
salt to taste
¼ cup white bread crumbs

Stir all ingredients together until the bread crumbs are dissolved and the sauce is smooth. Serve with hot fish, and it's particularly lovely with pompano, boiled beef and ham.

SAUCE PIQUANTE

2 small onions, chopped
1 cup oil
1 cup red wine
½ teaspoon oregano

½ teaspoon rosemary
1 clove garlic, crushed
5 tablespoons tarragon vinegar

Shake all ingredients and serve with cold meat.

SAUCE RÉMOULADE I

1½ cups mayonnaise
1 hard-cooked egg yolk, riced
2 tablespoons brown mustard
2 tablespoons chopped capers
1 small onion, chopped
1 tablespoon chopped chervil

1 tablespoon chopped parsley
1 tablespoon chopped tarragon
1 tablespoon anchovy paste
2 tablespoons chopped dill pickle
pepper to taste

Stir egg yolk into mayonnaise until it is smooth. Add all other ingredients and season to taste. Serve with cold roast beef, baked fish, cauliflower or mushrooms.

SAUCE RÉMOULADE II

To the above Sauce Rémoulade I, add 2 tablespoons Madeira wine and omit 2 tablespoons chopped capers.

SAUCE ST. VINCENT

To the above Sauce Rémoulade I, add enough white wine to stir into a thin sauce, correct seasoning.

SAUCE RÉMOULADE III

1 cup mayonnaise
1 hard-cooked egg yolk
1 small onion, chopped
2 tablespoons capers, chopped
½ small dill pickle, chopped

1 teaspoon mustard
1 teaspoon anchovy paste
2 tablespoons minced parsley
2 tablespoons white wine

Stir egg yolk into mayonnaise until it is smooth. Add all other ingredients and season to taste.

Variation: Add 3 tablespoons tomato catsup and 2 tablespoons Madeira, and omit white wine.

SAUCE RUSSE I

Add ¼ cup grated horse radish to Sauce Rémoulade.

SAUCE RUSSE II

3 tablespoons oil	3 tablespoons chopped chives
2 tablespoons vinegar	1 teaspoon chopped dill
3 tablespoons black caviar	salt and pepper to taste
3 tablespoons chopped parsley	

Stir oil and vinegar with salt and pepper until creamy, add caviar and herbs, and serve with meat or fish.

SAUCE RAVIGOTE

1 cup mayonnaise	1 tablespoon chopped chervil
3 tablespoons chopped dill pickle	1 tablespoon chopped parsley
2 tablespoons chopped shallots	1 tablespoon chopped capers
1 tablespoon chopped tarragon	1 tablespoon anchovy paste

Stir all ingredients together and serve with fish, cold meats, salads or vegetables.

ALBANY SAUCE

(in electric blender)

1 peeled cucumber, chopped	¼ cup jellied Madrilene
1 tablespoon tarragon vinegar	¼ cup cream
1 teaspoon anchovy paste	1 pinch each sugar, paprika and
2 teaspoons chutney, chopped	pepper
2 small gherkins, chopped (or 1 tablespoon sweet pickle relish)	2 drops vegetable green
	1 cup mayonnaise

Mix all ingredients or blend them in electric blender until a smooth sauce is obtained. Chill and serve with melon-ball cocktail, cold meat or fish.

HOT STEAK SAUCE

¼ cup dry mustard   ¼ cup fresh grated horse radish
½ cup tomato catsup

Stir mustard into catsup until smooth. Add horse radish and serve at once with steak or hamburgers.

SAUCE VERDI

1 cup mayonnaise   ¼ cup chopped dill pickle
½ cup sour cream   3 drops green food color
¼ cup chopped chives   salt and pepper to taste

Beat mayonnaise and sour cream together, add all other ingredients and serve with cold chicken, vegetables, salads, eggs in aspic, or pour it over boiled potatoes.

SAUCE VERTE

1 cup mayonnaise   1 tablespoon minced chives
6 spinach leaves, minced salt and pepper to taste
1 tablespoon minced parsley

Stir the finely minced spinach into the mayonnaise, including all the spinach juice extracted in mincing. Add parsley, chives, salt and pepper to taste. Serve with fish, vegetables, salads and meat.

MUSTARD SAUCE
(in electric blender)

2 tablespoons chopped tarragon   ½ teaspoon salt, or to taste
¼ cup brown or French mustard   ¼ teaspoon pepper
1 cup mayonnaise

Mix or blend all ingredients and serve with fish or meat.

ALEXANDRA SAUCE

3 hard-cooked eggs
½ cup mayonnaise
½ teaspoon English mustard
½ teaspoon salt
¼ teaspoon pepper

2 tablespoons tarragon vinegar
½ cup oil
1 tablespoon chopped pickle
1 tablespoon chopped, peeled
   truffles

Rice the egg yolks into a shallow bowl, stir in the mayonnaise, mustard, salt, pepper and vinegar. Stir in the oil little by little, adding only a few drops at a time, then increase as the sauce becomes smooth and creamy. Add pickle and truffles and egg whites cut into strips. Add salt to taste and serve cold with shrimps or, strangely enough, with a cold veal roast.

SAUCE FOR HAM
(in electric blender)

1 onion, chopped fine
½ cup mayonnaise
½ cup sour cream

3 tablespoons prepared mustard
salt and pepper to taste

Mix all ingredients or blend for ½ minute in electric blender, chill and serve with ham or tongue.

HORSE RADISH SAUCE
(Héssoise Sauce)

½ cup grated horse radish
1 cup sour cream
¼ cup fresh bread crumbs

3 tablespoons milk
sugar, salt and pepper to taste

Soak bread crumbs with milk, let stand 10 minutes. Add all other ingredients, whip until smooth and serve with hot or cold fish or meat.

SAUCE ESPAGNOLE

1 cup mayonnaise
⅓ cup chopped ham
1 teaspoon paprika

1 teaspoon mustard
1 clove garlic, crushed
salt and pepper to taste

Mix all ingredients, chill and serve with cold cauliflower, salads, meat or poultry.

BREAD SAUCE

3 slices white bread
½ cup milk
1 onion, finely chopped

salt and pepper to taste
1 cup whipped cream

Remove crusts from bread and soak in milk. Peel and finely chop onion and blend with bread and milk until smooth, season and chill. Fold in whipped cream and correct seasoning. Serve with meats, very good with game birds, especially pheasant.

GAME BIRD SAUCE

¼ cup catsup
2 tablespoons vinegar
2 tablespoons oil

salt and pepper to taste
2 shallots, minced
1 tablespoon prepared mustard

Stir all ingredients and serve with any cold game bird.

AGRO DOLCE

3 tablespoons brown sugar
⅓ cup white raisins
⅓ cup red raisins
3 tablespoons chopped blanched
    almonds

2 tablespoons chopped orange peel
2 tablespoons chopped lemon peel
2 tablespoons chopped capers
1 cup vinegar

Mix all ingredients, set aside for 2 hours. Heat and serve with ham or tongue.

AVOCADO SAUCE

1 avocado pear	1 teaspoon lemon juice
2 tablespoons chopped onion	1 clove garlic, crushed
2 tablespoons mayonnaise	3 dashes Tabasco Sauce
2 tablespoons sour cream	salt and cayenne to taste

Peel and seed avocado pear and crush into a smooth paste. Add all other ingredients, and serve over sliced oranges, fruit salad or green salad.

ANCHOVY SAUCE I

1 tablespoon anchovy paste	2 tablespoons cream
1 teaspoon prepared mustard	½ cup heavy cream
1 pinch each paprika and pepper	

Work anchovy paste, mustard, pepper and paprika into a paste with cream. Whip heavy cream and add paste during last minute of whipping. Serve with boiled salmon.

ANCHOVY SAUCE II

12 fillets of anchovy	4 hard-cooked eggs
2 tablespoons tarragon vinegar	3 tablespoons chopped parsley
3 tablespoons olive oil	1 tablespoon oregano
1 crushed garlic clove	1 tablespoon capers, chopped

Sieve or blend anchovies into a paste with vinegar and oil. Rice egg yolks into the mixture and stir until smooth, add all other ingredients and thin to preferred consistency with half vinegar and half water. Chill and serve with hot or cold meat or fish dishes.

This will make you thirsty, and what could be pleasanter than that?

EXTRA APPLE SAUCE

1 jar thick apple sauce
½ cup brown bread crumbs
6 toasted salted almonds, **chopped**
1 chopped onion

slivered outside rind of 1 orange
2 tablespoons wine
2 tablespoons vinegar
salt and pepper to taste

Mix and serve hot with meat.

BIGARADE SAUCE

1 orange
3 lumps sugar
½ cup currant jelly
¼ cup port wine

2 shallots, chopped
½ teaspoon prepared **mustard**
salt and pepper and cayenne to
taste

Grate orange rind over sugar and crush with a wooden spoon. Add juice of orange and remaining ingredients. Stir over hot water until jelly is melted. Serve with game or duck.

SAUCE EPICURIENNE

½ cup mayonnaise
¼ cup cream
2 tablespoons chopped chutney
1 tablespoon tarragon vinegar

½ cucumber, ground
1 teaspoon chopped gherkin
1 teaspoon anchovy paste
salt, pepper and sugar to taste

Mix all ingredients, chill and serve with meat, fish, asparagus or artichoke.

CAMBRIDGE SAUCE

3 hard-cooked egg yolks, riced
3 tablespoons oil
2 tablespoons tarragon vinegar
1 tablespoon capers, chopped
1 tablespoon anchovy paste
1 tablespoon chopped dill

1 tablespoon chopped tarragon
1 teaspoon each French and
    English mustard
pepper to taste
1 tablespoon chopped parsley

Pound and stir yolks with oil and vinegar until smooth. Add all other ingredients except parsley, stir well and chill. Serve dusted with the chopped parsley. Excellent with cold meat.

SAUCE MOUSSELINE

1 cup mayonnaise
⅔ cup whipped cream

3 tablespoons lemon juice
1 pinch salt

Stir lemon juice into mayonnaise and fold in whipped cream. Serve with hot vegetables or meat.

ONION SAUCE FOR FISH

2 medium onions, cut into paper-
    thin slices and separated
¼ pound salt butter

¼ cup finely chopped parsley
salt and pepper to taste

Melt butter, but do not let it brown, add all other ingredients and serve with any hot fish.

SHALLOT SAUCE

(to serve with steak)

1 cup shallots, peeled and chopped
½ pound hot melted salt butter

½ cup finely chopped parsley
salt to taste

Add shallots and parsley to hot butter, salt to taste, and serve with steaks, roast beef or just with hot baked potatoes. The last is the best.

FRENCH MUSTARD SAUCE

4 hard-cooked eggs, riced
2 tablespoons vinegar
1 tablespoon lemon juice
⅓ cup oil

3 tablespoons French mustard
    (Dijon)
½ teaspoon sugar
¼ teaspoon white pepper
salt to taste

Stir into a creamy sauce and serve with boiled beef or any boiled fish.

MALTA MAYONNAISE

1 cup mayonnaise	3 tablespoons orange juice
¼ cup cold ground ham	1 tablespoon port wine

Mix all ingredients and serve with hot or cold boiled asparagus.

MINT SAUCE

1 cup vinegar	1 cup finely chopped mint
2 teaspoons sugar, or to taste	

Dissolve sugar in vinegar. Add mint and steep for at least 2 hours. Serve with lamb, veal or chicken.

HOT APRICOT SAUCE

1 cup apricot jam	½ cup almonds, blanched and
1 cup apricot nectar	slivered
3 tablespoons apricot brandy	

Melt jam and nectar over hot water. Add brandy and almonds and serve hot over fruit, puddings or ice cream.

This sauce goes far to make a bland cold pudding or plain vanilla ice cream into a gala dessert. The fact is that it is one of those sauces that can be served for itself alone, with ice cream as an excuse for having it!

THE COLONEL'S LADY

1 cup dark brown sugar	3 tablespoons whiskey or brandy
½ cup butter	½ cup half-whipped cream
1 egg yolk	

Cream butter and sugar, beat in egg yolk and whiskey. Gradually beat in cream, chill and serve with puddings or fruit.

WHIPPED BRANDY CREAM
(for Christmas puddings and pies)

1 cup cream	grated rind of 1 lemon
2 tablespoons sugar	¼ cup brandy

Whip cream with sugar and lemon rind until almost stiff. Slowly whip in brandy and serve immediately with plum pudding or mince pie.

SAUCE MELBA
(in electric blender)

1 package frozen raspberries	½ teaspoon vanilla
¼ cup powdered sugar	

Defrost raspberries. Blend until smooth with sugar, add vanilla and serve.

ORANGE SAUCE

1 jar orange marmalade	½ teaspoon almond extract
2 jiggers curaçao	½ cup blanched slivered almonds

Melt marmalade over hot water, add all other ingredients and serve hot or cold with ice cream, puddings and mousses.

Pour a thin layer of it over an open apple tart, or serve it with freshly stewed apples.

BROWN SUGAR HARD SAUCE

½ cup butter, creamed	1 tablespoon rum
¾ cup light brown sugar	

Beat sugar and rum into butter until light and creamy. Chill until needed. Serve with hot puddings or Brown Betty.

CHOCOLATE SAUCE I

4 squares chocolate
¼ cup sugar

1 cup hot water
½ cup heavy cream

Place first 3 ingredients in the top of a double boiler over boiling water. When the chocolate is melted, stir it well until it is smooth. Cool the sauce and when it is cold beat in heavy cream to taste or fold in whipped cream to taste.

CHOCOLATE SAUCE II

½ pound sweet chocolate

1 cup water

Melt chocolate in the water over low heat and beat until smooth. Reduce water and substitute heavy cream if desired. Flavor with vanilla, or use coffee instead of water.

CHOCOLATE RUM SAUCE

1 package chocolate rum wafers
1 cup strong hot coffee

1 teaspoon vanilla

Melt chocolate wafers over hot water. Stir in coffee and vanilla. Beat well and serve hot or cold with ice cream or vanilla pudding.

CHOCOLATE MINT SAUCE

1 package chocolate mint wafers
3 peppermint wafers or
    after-dinner mints

⅓ cup cream
1 pinch salt

Melt chocolate wafers over hot water, stir in the after-dinner mints or peppermint wafers until they are dissolved. Add cream and salt, and beat until smooth. Serve hot or cold with ice cream or puddings.

Remember the child that wanted chocolate sauce on everything? He's grown up now—for all you know he's your husband!

CHANTILLY CREAM

1 cup whipped cream   1 teaspoon vanilla
¼ cup powdered sugar

Add sugar and vanilla to whipped cream, during last minute of whipping.

RUM PUNCH SAUCE

½ pound butter   ¼ cup rum
½ cup sherry   ½ lemon, juice and grated rind
2 jiggers brandy   ¼ cup sugar or to taste

Heat all ingredients over hot water, beating until smooth. Serve hot with puddings and ice cream or fruit.

RUM SAUCE

½ cup butter, creamed   ½ cup rum
½ cup sugar   ¼ cup chopped walnuts

Stir sugar and rum into the creamed butter. Add walnuts, chill and serve with hot puddings. It might even bring a Brown Betty to life. You can also serve the sauce with hot stewed pears.

It is not a question of what to serve the sauce with. Just what to pass with the sauce.

SHERRY OR PORT WINE SAUCE

1 cup butter
½ cup hot sherry or port wine

1 jigger brandy
2 tablespoons sugar, or to taste

Soften butter over warm water until it can be beaten. Beat in sherry, brandy and sugar and serve with Christmas pudding, ice cream, mousse. Or very good over chilled melon balls or pineapple chunks.

HARD SAUCE

¼ cup butter
⅔ cup powdered sugar

½ teaspoon lemon juice
½ teaspoon vanilla or brandy

Cream the butter, slowly add the sugar and flavoring and chill before serving. Serve with hot puddings—it's the only reason why children eat puddings.

APRICOT MOUSSELINE SAUCE

½ cup cream
1 recipe Hot Apricot Sauce (see page 181)

2 tablespoons additional apricot brandy

Cool Apricot Sauce, half-whip cream, mix with sauce and flavor with additional brandy. Serve with hot chocolate, apricot or vanilla pudding.

BRANDY ORANGE SAUCE

½ cup butter, creamed
½ cup powdered sugar
½ cup brandy

2 tablespoons grated orange rind
2 tablespoons orange juice

Stir all ingredients into the creamed butter. Chill and serve with warm apple pie, fig pudding or deep dish apple pie.

ORANGE HARD SAUCE

½ cup butter
¾ cup four-X sugar
2 tablespoons cream
3 tablespoons orange juice

2 tablespoons finely chopped
   candied orange peel
1 tablespoon orange liqueur,
   Grand Marnier or curaçao

Cream butter and sugar, beat in cream and slowly add fruit juice, peel and liqueur. Chill before serving.

LEMON HARD SAUCE

Follow recipe for Orange Hard Sauce, substituting lemon juice and rind for orange juice and omitting orange liqueur.

Serve either sauce with fig pudding, plum pudding or any cooked apple pudding or deep dish pie.

PINEAPPLE SAUCE

1 can pineapple chunks
1 cup red currant jelly

1 jigger kirsch

Melt currant jelly over hot water, add pineapple and kirsch, and serve hot or cold over ice cream, mousses or over stewed pears or peaches.

CHAPTER 13. *Desserts*

THE dessert course is the one that usually troubles the hostess or housewife most. If she can think of something that would be just the right thing to end the meal with, she rarely has enough time to make it, but usually she cannot even think of it.

A meal that made a deep impression on me, more from disappointment than from satisfaction, was a Sunday luncheon served by a well-known hostess. The first course and soup were delicious, the roast and vegetables were perfection. The meal and the conversation progressed to the point where the feeling of well-being needed only to end well to be another of the hostess's memorable meals.

There did not necessarily have to be a heavy or an elaborate dessert, only something to round out the pleasure and remove the lingering saddle of lamb.

At the moment of expectation the hostess arose, "lifted" the table and said, "I *simply* could not think of a dessert!"

The NO COOKING COOKBOOK can be of real help here. It may be necessary to whip cream or peel fruit, but all other effort stops after the preparation of the ingredients. There is no cooking, no other complicated procedure.

Some of the desserts require time for chilling or heating, but on

187

the whole the non-cooked desserts are effortless and more interesting and inviting than many elaborately baked or frozen ones. (Bonus: most of them are also much more slimming!)

FILLED ORANGES

2 oranges
1 cup strawberries
4 whole strawberries

sugar to taste
2 teaspoons maraschino

Halve oranges, scoop out the meat and pulp. Remove pits and mix meat and juice with roughly crushed strawberries. Add sugar and maraschino and refill orange halves. Top with whole strawberries and serve chilled.

ORANGE MACAROONS

4 oranges, peeled and sliced
¼ cup confectioners sugar

2 cups crushed macaroons
1 cup cream, whipped

Lay sugared and chilled orange slices into a serving dish. Sprinkle with half the macaroons, cover with whipped cream and sprinkle remaining macaroons over the cream. Oranges may be flavored with orange liqueur, curaçao, Grand Marnier or Triple Sec.

ICED ORANGE ICE

4 large oranges
1½ pints orange ice

lemon leaves or mint sprigs

Cut a lid from the stem end of oranges. Hollow out the shell and the lid and pack each orange full of orange ice. Replace lid to simulate a whole orange and chill in freezing compartment or coldest part of refrigerator until needed. Serve on lemon leaves or with sprigs of mint.

ORANGE SNOW

2 eggs, separated
2 teaspoons sugar

2 tablespoons cream
juice of 2 oranges

Beat yolks with sugar, cream and fruit juice. Fold in stiffly beaten whites and serve at once.

AMBROSIA

6 large oranges
¼ cup powdered sugar
1 package of grated coconut

2 jiggers curaçao or any orange liqueur

Cut oranges in half, take out sections with a knife or spoon, keeping them as nearly intact as possible. Combine with sugar and coconut and refill 8 of the half shells, mounding the filling high. Add the liqueur, chill and serve 2 halves to each portion. If oranges are very large, recipe can be cut in half.

PINEAPPLE GLACÉ

1 pineapple
1 quart orange ice
¼ cup confectioners sugar or to
taste

2 tablespoons orange curaçao
1 tablespoon kirsch

Cut top from pineapple, scoop out interior, fill with orange ice, put on top and freeze. Crush pineapple pulp with sugar and liqueurs and serve with the pineapple.

MINTED PINEAPPLE

2 10½-ounce cans pineapple
chunks
3 tablespoons chopped fresh mint

3 tablespoons white crème de
menthe

Drain pineapple chunks, divide over four coupe glasses, pour crème de menthe over them and dust with chopped mint.

NEIGE D'ANANA
(Pineapple Snow)

1 small pineapple or 1 can crushed pineapple	1 cup cream
	¼ cup sugar
4 egg whites	¼ cup brandy

Have all ingredients very cold. Peel and grate pineapple, or use canned. Beat egg whites very stiff, adding sugar gradually. Whip the cream stiff and fold into the whites. Add the pineapple and its juice gradually. Substitute brandy to taste for part of the juice. Mound in dessert glasses and chill until needed.

FLAMING BANANAS AND ICE CREAM

6 bananas, sliced	½ cup heavy rum, warmed
¼ cup confectioners sugar	1 quart vanilla ice cream

Sugar bananas, add warm rum, flame and pour over ice cream.

BANANAS AND KIRSCH

4 bananas, sliced	sugar to taste
2 tablespoons kirsch	6 candied cherries, chopped
½ cup cream, whipped	

Flavor whipped cream with kirsch and sugar to taste, spread over bananas and dust with chopped cherries.

EGG-BRANDY SALAD

4 bananas, sliced thin	3 tablespoons brandy
juice and grated rind of 1½ lemons	sugar to taste
3 egg yolks	

Marinate bananas in lemon juice, turning frequently. Drain off lemon juice and cover with brandy beaten into yolks until light and creamy and sugared to taste.

BRANDIED GRAPEFRUIT
(in electric blender)

2 grapefruit
½ cup fresh or canned grapefruit
    juice
2 tablespoons sugar

1 jigger brandy
2 tablespoons maraschino
1½ cup shaved ice

Prepare grapefruit by taking out center and loosening sections. Retain all juice and chill fruit. Just before serving blend all other ingredients and mound the mixture into the grapefruit hollows. Serve at once.

STRAWBERRIES

1 basket hulled strawberries
¼ cup rum
¼ cup walnuts chopped fine

¼ cup powdered sugar
½ cup cream, whipped

Pour rum over chilled strawberries, dust with nuts and sugar and serve with whipped cream.

STRAWBERRIES AND CREAM

¾ cup sour cream
1 small cream cheese

¼ cup sugar
1 basket strawberries

Whip sour cream with cheese and sugar until smooth. Arrange unhulled strawberries on 4 plates with mounds of powdered sugar and cheese cream on each plate.

STRAWBERRIES AND SOUR CREAM

1 pound strawberries, hulled
½ cup sugar

1½ cups sour cream
¾ cup bread crumbs

Slice strawberries and sprinkle with sugar. Whip sour cream with bread crumbs and add strawberries with their juice. Serve with sugar.

STRAWBERRY MIEL

2 quart baskets strawberries   1 can walnuts, chopped
½ cup thin honey

Hull strawberries, dribble honey over them and dust with walnuts. Serve very cold.

STRAWBERRY AMBROSIA

1 pineapple   powdered sugar to taste
1 quart strawberries, hulled and   3 tablespoons lime juice, or to taste
   sliced   1 can shredded coconut

Cut pineapple in half lengthwise, cut out meat, remove core and dice or cube it, leaving two ½-inch-thick pineapple shells. Sugar pineapple and strawberries to taste, mix with half the coconut and refill pineapple shells with the fruit. Dust with remaining coconut and serve chilled, sprinkled with lime juice.

BACHELORS' DELIGHT

2 cups hulled strawberries   4 splits iced champagne
2 tablespoons sugar

Fill 4 beakers half full of sugared strawberries. Pour over chilled champagne and serve at once.

STRAWBERRIES CREOLE

2 cups strawberries, sliced   1 jigger Grand Marnier
2 cups crushed pineapple, drained   1 pineapple, peeled, cored and
½ cup powdered sugar   sliced
1 jigger kirsch   grated rind of 1 orange

Mix first 5 ingredients and chill, turning several times. Serve in the center of a chilled bowl surrounded by overlapping, halved pineapple slices. Sprinkle with sugar and orange rind and serve very cold.

STRAWBERRIES CARDINAL

4 cups strawberries
2 cups raspberries
⅔ cup powdered sugar

1 teaspoon lemon juice
¼ cup shredded blanched almonds

Hull and chill strawberries, press raspberries through a sieve or "blend" with sugar and lemon juice into a thick purée and chill. Serve the strawberries in a chilled bowl with the raspberry sauce poured over and sprinkled with almonds.

HONEYDEW MELON

1 honeydew melon
2 cans pineapple cubes

1 teaspoon ground ginger
1 teaspoon ground cloves

Drain juice from pineapple and heat it with ginger and cloves. Cut lid from melon, scoop out seeds and pour in warm juice. Set in refrigerator for 2 hours, drain and fill with chilled pineapple. Return as much juice as there is room for. Serve as cold as possible.

MELON BALLS

3 cups cantaloupe and watermelon
    balls
2 jiggers kirsch

½ cup sugar
1 tablespoon chopped mint
1 tablespoon crème de menthe

Mix, chill and serve.

FILLED MELON

1 honeydew melon
1 cantaloupe cut into melon balls
1 cup seedless grapes
1 cup blueberries

1 cup strawberries
¼ cup diced candied orange rind
¼ cup diced candied cherries
flavor with liqueur if desired

Cut lid from honeydew melon, remove seeds and scoop out meat. Drain and chill melon shell. Blend or crush meat of honeydew with sugar to taste. Fill melon shell with fresh and candied fruit and add the sweetened honeydew sauce. Cover with lid and serve melon on lemon leaves.

MELON GLACÉ

1 large cantaloupe
1 quart vanilla ice cream

1½ cups Apricot Sauce (see page 181)
¼ cup slivered almonds

Cut lid from iced cantaloupe, hollow out interior, fill with ice cream, put on lid and place in freezer. Dice melon meat, mix with Apricot Sauce and almonds. Serve by cutting wedges of melon with the ice cream filling and pass melon sauce separately.

FRENCH PLUMS

2 jars or cans stewed red plums
3 tablespoons kirsch

2 tablespoons slivered lemon peel

Heat plums in their own syrup, add kirsch and the finely slivered yellow outside rind of lemons. Serve warm or cold.

PLUMS IN COINTREAU

1 can red plums, drained
1 can kumquats, drained
2 oranges, thinly sliced
2 tablespoons raisins
¼ cup brandy
2 tablespoons brown sugar

½ teaspoon vanilla
¼ teaspoon cinnamon
¼ teaspoon powdered cloves
1 pinch salt
Cointreau to taste

Arrange plums, kumquats, orange slices and raisins in serving dish, combine all other ingredients with Cointreau to taste, pour over and chill before serving.

GREENGAGES

2 jars greengage plums
2 tablespoons kirsch

1 tablespoon rum
2 tablespoons slivered lemon peel

Prepare as French Plums (see page 194) and serve cold. Very good with meat course.

HOT CHERRIES

1 can pitted black cherries, heated
½ cup slivered blanched almonds
½ cup cookie or macaroon crumbs
½ cup raisins

¼ cup sugar
¼ teaspoon cinnamon
1 cup cream

Drain all but ½ cup juice from cherries, add all other ingredients and serve with cream.

STUFFED CHERRIES

2 pounds large black cherries
1 package shelled hazel nuts
   (filberts)

¼ cup powdered sugar
1 jigger maraschino
1 cup cream, half whipped

Pit cherries, and retain all juice. Press hazel nut or a half hazel nut into each cherry, sugar and chill. Add maraschino and serve with cream.

If you have time and patience, all this is very well. If you don't, use canned pitted cherries and either stuff them or just combine them with chopped hazel nuts. It's the combination which tastes good. The stuffing isn't necessary.

COMPOTE OF CHERRIES AND ALMONDS

1½ pounds sweet cherries
1 cup sugar, or to taste
1 can slivered almonds
3 tablespoons maraschino

4 stale macaroons, crushed
1 cup sour cream beaten with 3
   tablespoons sugar

Pit cherries over a bowl to catch all cherry juice. Add sugar to cherries and juice and stir well. Set in refrigerator for ½ hour. Add almonds, maraschino and macaroon crumbs and serve with sweetened sour cream.

FRUIT CARDINAL

(in electric blender)

Canned peaches, pears or apricots may be prepared in this way.

1-pound can peach halves	1 jigger kirsch
½ teaspoon vanilla	½ cup toasted slivered almonds
1 package raspberries puréed in blender	

Drain peaches of all but ½ cup syrup. Flavor with vanilla, add almonds and chill. Serve with raspberry sauce, flavored with kirsch.

RASPBERRY WHIP

1 basket raspberries	8 ladyfingers or sponge cake fingers
2 egg whites	
1 cup four-X sugar	1 cup raspberry sauce (see Fruit Cardinal)

Whisk egg whites with sugar until half stiff, add raspberries and continue to whisk until stiff. Mound on a dish and chill. Serve surrounded by ladyfingers and pass raspberry sauce separately.

RASPBERRIES ROMANOFF

2 quarts raspberries	confectioners sugar to taste
juice of ½ orange	1 pint vanilla ice cream
2 ounces Cointreau or Triple Sec	1 cup cream, whipped
2 ounces kirsch	

Pour orange juice and liqueur over berries, sweeten if necessary and set in refrigerator. Beat ice cream with rotary or electric beater until it is smooth and soft, fold in whipped cream, pour over berries and serve. Stir berries and cream only as they are served.

KADOTA FIGS

(in electric blender)

1 jar figs
½ cup orange marmalade

½ cup chopped Brazil nuts

Blend syrup from figs with marmalade into a smooth sauce. Chill figs in sauce and serve dusted with Brazil nuts.

MUSTAPHA PEARS

4 egg yolks
⅔ cup brown sugar
1 cup heavy cream, heated

1 teaspoon vanilla
6 pears, stewed or canned, heated
   in their own juice

Beat yolks and sugar until light and creamy, add cream gradually, flavor with vanilla and pour over drained pears.

PEARS HÉLÈNE

4 stewed whole pears
1 pint vanilla ice cream

1 cup hot Chocolate Sauce (see
   page 183)
¼ cup chopped toasted almonds

Divide ice cream into 4 glass dessert dishes, place 1 pear on each and dust with almonds. Pass Chocolate Sauce separately.

PEARS MARY GARDEN

4 stewed whole pears
⅔ cup Sauce Melba (see page 182)
1 glass crystallized cherries, chopped

1 cup cream
1 teaspoon vanilla
2 tablespoons confectioners sugar

Chop cherries, mix them with Melba Sauce and pour over 4

pears arranged in 4 dessert dishes. Whip cream with vanilla and sugar and pass separately.

APPLE SAUCE

1 large jar apple sauce
½ cup white wine
¼ cup sugar

½ cup toasted almonds, chopped
½ cup sour cream

Mix, chill and serve.

APPLE SAUCE

(in electric blender)

1 can apple sauce
1 tablespoon honey

½ lemon, juice and grated rind
1 tablespoon brandy

Place in blender, blend only long enough to mix. Chill and serve with cheese wedges.

APPLES MARIETTA

1 jar stewed apples
1 can chestnut purée
2 tablespoons rum

¼ cup cream
⅔ cup Apricot Sauce (see page 181)
sugar to taste

Arrange stewed apples in serving dish, beat rum and cream into chestnut purée and sugar to taste. Pour over apples and serve with Apricot Sauce.

PEACH FREEZE

1-pound can peach halves
¼ cup sugar
½ cup peach syrup from can

½ cup unsweetened orange juice
2 tablespoons lemon juice
¼ cup chopped pecans

Chill peaches. Dissolve sugar in syrup and orange juice and pour into refrigerator tray. Set control at lowest temperature and freeze until firm, stirring every half hour. Set temperature back to medium. Serve by spooning ice over peach halves and dusting with pecans.

PEACH CREAM

1 cup heavy cream, whipped
3 peaches, peeled and very thinly sliced
½ teaspoon vanilla

2 teaspoons heavy rum
3 tablespoons confectioners sugar
½ cup shredded coconut

Whip cream and flavor with vanilla and rum. Fold sugared peaches and coconut into cream and serve at once in chilled glasses.

COLD APRICOTS

1 can apricots, drained
6 dry macaroons, crushed
2 egg yolks

½ cup heavy cream, whipped
2 tablespoons powdered sugar
½ teaspoon vanilla

Whip cream, fold in egg yolks, sugar and vanilla, spread over apricots and dust with macaroon crumbs.

APRICOTS AND BRANDY

1 can apricots, drained
½ cup slivered almonds
½ cup cream, whipped

2 tablespoons apricot brandy
1 tablespoon sugar

Fold brandy and sugar into whipped cream, pour over apricots in serving dish and dust with slivered almonds.

APRICOT MOUSSE

1½ cups powdered sugar
½ cup butter
2 eggs
1 cup cream, whipped

1 cup apricot pulp
½ cup chopped nuts
8 ounces vanilla wafers, crushed
⅔ cup Apricot Sauce (see page 181)

Beat sugar and butter until creamy and white, beat in eggs one after the other, fold in whipped cream, apricot and nuts. Spread crushed wafers in a shallow mold, pour in mousse and freeze, in coldest part of refrigerator or in freezer. Slice and serve with Apricot Sauce.

APRICOT SNOW

¾ cup cold apricot nectar
¾ cup instant non-fat dry milk
    crystals
juice and grated rind of 1 lemon

1 tablespoon apricot brandy or
    brandy
3 tablespoons sugar

Whip first 2 ingredients until half whipped, add flavoring and continue beating. Add sugar gradually until mixture is stiff. Serve in chilled dessert glasses.

APRICOT AMBROSIA
(in electric blender)

Blend or sieve 1 large can drained apricots until smooth. Chill and turn into an iced serving dish. Cover with lattice lines of piped whipped cream and fill each diamond with a strawberry marinated in kirsch and rolled in sugar. Pink sugar, which can be bought commercially, makes strawberries very pretty.

PORTO PEACHES

6 peaches
sugar

port wine

Skin and slice peaches, place in a dish and dust them with sugar. Cover with port wine and set in refrigerator for 1 hour before serving.

PEACHES ALEXANDRA

1 cup strawberries	4 large canned peach halves
½ cup powdered sugar	1½ pints vanilla ice cream

Purée fresh or frozen strawberries through a sieve or in a blender. If fresh strawberries are used, add powdered sugar to taste. Serve peach halves on vanilla ice cream with blended strawberries poured over.

PEACH MELBA

(Devised by Escoffier in honor of Nelly Melba, soprano. Her real name was Mitchell, but even Escoffier could not have made a Pêche Helen Mitchell famous.)

2 large ripe peaches	1 pound fresh raspberries, or 1
1½ pints French vanilla ice cream	package frozen raspberries,
1 8-ounce jar currant jelly	thawed

Use canned peaches if fresh ones are not in season. Press raspberries and currant jelly through a fine sieve, stir until smooth. Arrange peach halves, round-side-up on ice cream in 4 crystal dessert dishes. Pour over sauce and serve with the slivered almonds from the cracked peach pits. If possible, crack 10 more peach pits, extract the almond, draw off the skin and sliver. Fresh green almonds may also be used.

COFFEE PRUNE WHIP

1½ cups canned prunes	1 pinch salt
⅓ cup powdered sugar	2 tablespoons strong coffee
½ teaspoon grated orange rind	1 cup cream, whipped
¼ teaspoon cinnamon	maraschino to taste

Pit and crush prunes with next five ingredients, whip mixture until light and fluffy. Whip cream until half stiff and gradually whip prunes into cream. Chill and serve in glasses which have been moistened with a few drops of maraschino.

PRUNES WITH PECANS

2 jars stewed prunes
1 orange, juice and slivered rind
¼ cup dark rum
½ cup brown sugar

¼ teaspoon each ground
　　cinnamon, cloves and ginger
1 pinch of salt
½ cup chopped pecans

Mix orange juice, rum, sugar and spices. Pour over drained prunes, dust with orange rind and nuts and serve chilled.

GINGER KUMQUATS

1 jar kumquats in syrup
1 jar orange marmalade
¼ cup preserved ginger, ground
¼ teaspoon ground cinnamon

¼ teaspoon ground cloves
¼ teaspoon ground ginger
1 cup cream, whipped

Melt orange marmalade over hot water. Add all other ingredients, decreasing preserved ginger to taste. Stir well. Cool and chill. Serve with whipped cream.

COUPES

Coupes are a combination of ice creams, ices, fruits, sauces and whipped cream. They can be prepared in tall champagne glasses or cups and served immediately, or they can be prepared in advance and chilled in freezer or coldest part of refrigerator. If prepared in thin glasses they should not be placed in freezer for more than 1 hour.

COUPE AU MARRONS

1 jar marrons in syrup
1 pint vanilla ice cream

½ cup whipped cream

Put 4 tablespoons marrons into 4 coupe glasses. Half-fill with ice cream, add more marrons and fill with ice cream. Top with whipped cream on marrons.

COUPE ST. JACQUES

2 cups cold fresh fruit cocktail in-
    cluding orange sections
1 jigger kirsch

1 pint lemon ice
4 small scoops strawberry ice cream

Retain 4 orange sections from the fruit cocktail. Half-fill 4 coupe glasses with fruit. Add kirsch and cover with lemon ice. Top with strawberry ice cream and end with orange section on top.

COUPE MARIE

2 cups sliced peaches
1 pint orange water ice

1 jigger curaçao

Half-fill 4 coupe glasses with peaches. Top with orange ice and pour a little curaçao over. Decorate top with a peach slice.

COUPE MARIE LOUISE

1 basket strawberries
1 jigger curaçao

1 pint strawberry ice cream
½ cup whipped cream

Half-fill 4 coupe glasses with strawberries, setting 4 aside for the top. Add curaçao and top with strawberry ice cream. Decorate top with whipped cream and center with strawberry.

COUPE COMTESSE

2 cups sliced peaches, canned or
    fresh
¼ cup Melba Sauce (see page 182)

1 pint vanilla ice cream
2 tablespoons chopped almonds

Half-fill 4 coupe glasses with sliced peaches, pour over Melba Sauce and top with ice cream and almonds.

MOUSSE AU CHOCOLAT

1 square bitter chocolate
4 squares sweetened chocolate
1 tablespoon butter
2 tablespoons sugar

water
4 eggs, separated
chopped walnuts, optional

Melt chocolate with sugar and butter over hot water. Beat in just enough water to make into a smooth thick paste. Cool, beat in egg yolks and fold in egg whites. Pour into individual glasses or bowl, sprinkle with chopped walnuts, and chill at least 3 hours.

BUDAPEST CHOCOLATE
(serves eight)

Mix in rotation:

½ pound semi-sweet chocolate
    melted over hot water or in
    double boiler
1¼ cups sugar
1 tablespoon vanilla

2 tablespoons rum
½ cup cream
5 egg yolks
5 egg whites, beaten stiff
1 cup cream, whipped

Chill and serve.

APPLE PUDDING

2 cups corn flakes
2 cups sweet cookie crumbs
1 large jar apple sauce
½ cup sugar

½ cup raisins
½ cup slivered almonds
1 pint vanilla ice cream

Crush corn flakes with a rolling pin and mix with cookie crumbs. In a deep dish, arrange layers of these crumbs with layers of apple sauce sprinkled with raisins and almonds. Dust each layer with sugar and end with a layer of crumbs. Serve cold with softened vanilla ice cream, beaten until fluffy with an electric or rotary beater.

RUM CREAM

4 egg yolks
½ cup powdered sugar
2 tablespoons rum

1½ cups heavy cream, whipped
3 tablespoons grated semi-sweet
    chocolate

Beat egg yolks with sugar until they are light and creamy, add rum and fold in whipped cream. Pour into serving dish, chill and serve dusted with grated chocolate.

COLD COFFEE CREAM

3 egg yolks
3 tablespoons sugar
2 tablespoons strong coffee

1 tablespoon rum
3 egg whites, beaten stiff
¾ cup cream, whipped

Beat yolks with sugar until creamy, add coffee and rum and fold in egg whites and whipped cream. Chill and serve.

PARFAIT DE MIEL

¾ cup honey
4 eggs

2 cups cream, whipped

Heat honey to just under boiling, beat in 4 eggs. Continue to beat until the mixture is cold and thick. Fold in whipped cream, pour into a mold and freeze.

COEUR À LA CRÈME

1 cup cottage cheese, riced
1 8-ounce package cream cheese,
    riced
1 cup heavy cream, whipped

¼ cup powdered sugar
2 tablespoons cream
1 quart large strawberries

Beat cheeses together until they are smooth and light. Whip cream, gradually adding sugar and fold into cheese.

Line a small French heart-shaped basket with moistened cheese cloth. Press cheese into basket and refrigerate over night. Unmold and pour the cream over it. Surround with cold sweetened strawberries. Do not hull the strawberries.

PESTER CREAM

2 bars sweet chocolate	2 tablespoons sugar
2 tablespoons strong coffee	2 egg whites

Melt chocolate in coffee over hot water, whip well and set aside to cool. Beat eggs half stiff, gradually add sugar, beat until stiff and fold in chocolate. Serve at once in chilled dessert glasses.

SEVILLE CREAM

¼ cup orange marmalade, including peel	juice of ½ lemon
	sugar to taste
2 tablespoons brandy	2 cups chilled cream

Chop marmalade, then whip it with brandy, lemon juice and sugar. Add the mixture gradually to cream while whipping it stiff. Mound into a chilled serving dish and serve very cold.

SPANISH CREAM

1 tablespoon brandy	½ lemon, juice and grated rind
1 tablespoon drained orange marmalade, minced	2 cups heavy cream
	powdered sugar to taste

Mix first 3 ingredients, add gradually to half-whipped cream and continue to whip, adding sugar to taste until cream is stiff. Fill into chilled glasses, chill and serve.

ICE CREAM CAKE

4 individual sponge cake shells
1 pint chocolate ice cream
4 drops peppermint extract (may be
purchased at any drug store)

1 cup Chocolate Sauce
(see page 183)
½ cup chopped toasted almonds

Fill shells with ice cream and chill. Add peppermint to Chocolate Sauce, pour over shells and top with almonds. Serve at once.

ICE CREAM PIE

20 crisp chocolate crackers, crushed
¼ cup chopped pecans
¼ cup powdered sugar
⅓ cup butter, melted
1 quart vanilla ice cream

½ cup cream, whipped
12 half pecans
4 melted milk chocolate bars
¼ cup cream

Crush cracker crumbs, pecans and sugar together. Work into melted butter and press into bottom and sides of metal pie tin. Cover with ice cream, pack down well and place in freezing compartment of refrigerator. Turn gauge to coldest temperature for 2 hours, or place pie tin into freezer. Decorate with whipped cream and whole pecans. Serve with a sauce made of melted chocolate bars, beaten with cream.

LAYER CAKE

2 layers (prepared layer cake)
2 large cream cheeses, riced
2 squares sweet chocolate, grated
½ teaspoon vanilla
½ cup powdered sugar
3 tablespoons crème de cacao or
rum

grated rind of 1 orange
¼ cup heavy cream
½ cup chopped candied cherries
¼ cup chopped candied orange
rind

Stir riced cheese with chocolate, vanilla, sugar, liqueur, orange rind and enough heavy cream to make into a smooth frosting.

Fill and frost 2 plain cake layers and decorate top with candied fruit.

FROZEN EGG NOG

1 quart vanilla ice cream	2 cups whipped cream
½ cup heavy rum	nutmeg

Whip slightly softened ice cream with rum, fold in whipped cream, fill into parfait glasses, dust with nutmeg and serve at once.

BRANDY DELIGHT

6 hard-cooked egg yolks, riced	¼ cup slivered toasted almonds
½ cup butter	4 to 6 slices pound cake
½ cup confectioners sugar	(commercial)
1 teaspoon vanilla	brandy or sherry
8 stale macaroons, crushed	sugar to taste

Pound yolks into a smooth paste. Cream butter and beat in sugar and yolks until smooth; add vanilla. Cut 4 rounds out of pound cake slices with a cookie cutter. Arrange in dessert glasses, sprinkle generously with brandy or sherry and spread with half the cream. Cover with a second pound cake round, sprinkle again and cover with remaining cream and almonds. Mix macaroon crumbs with brandy and sugar to taste and spread over top. Set in refrigerator for as long as possible. It may be made the day before it is served.

BISCUIT TORTONI

3 eggs, separated	¾ cup crushed macaroons
1½ cups heavy cream, whipped	1 teaspoon vanilla
¾ cup powdered sugar	3 tablespoons sherry

Beat yolks and sugar until light and creamy, add sherry and vanilla. Beat egg whites stiff, whip the cream and fold it into the egg whites with ½ cup crushed macaroons. Gently fold in the yolk mixture and fill into paper cups or china ramekins. Dust with remaining macaroons and place in freezing compartment or freezer until firm.

SWEET CHEESE HEART

1 pound cream cheese
½ cup heavy cream
1 cup heavy cream whipped with
2 tablespoons powdered sugar
2 jiggers heavy rum

1 package frozen strawberries,
    thawed
1 package frozen raspberries,
    thawed
½ teaspoon vanilla

Beat cheese and cream until smooth. Fold in cream whipped with sugar and flavor with rum. Form into a ball, wrap in wet cheese cloth and refrigerate at least 3 hours. Unwrap and serve surrounded with drained strawberries. Blend raspberries into a sauce for 3 minutes, add vanilla and pour over strawberries.

FOOD FOR THE GODS I

1 loaf 2-day-old pumpernickel, or
    dark bread
1 cup pitted black cherries

¾ cup sugar
½ cup cherry jam
2 cups whipped cream

Crush dark bread or pumpernickel into crumbs. Mix with well-drained cherries and sugar. Mound on a serving dish, dot with cherry jam, mask with whipped cream and serve.

FOOD FOR THE GODS II

1¼ cups cream
½ cup sugar
2 cups stale dark bread crumbs or
    pumpernickel

¼ cup rum or maraschino syrup
3 macaroons, crushed

Whip cream, adding sugar gradually. Fold crumbs and syrup into cream and mound in a bowl. Sprinkle with macaroons.

CHAPTER 14.   *Icings*

CHILDREN, who always know what is best, leave the icing on the cake to the last. Adults, who forget what is best while they concentrate on what is best for them, are very apt to eat their cake and icing at the same time. There are even those who eat cake without icing and some who don't eat cake at all when they are at home, but eat great towering layers when they are out. Their theory is that the pastry chef should go through the pains of boiling the sugar and beating the icing into glossy perfection. They leave the hard part to the professionals and keep the pleasant part, the eating, for themselves. It is not easy to make a good icing and very few cooks can produce that beautiful, mysterious, enamel-like thing called fondant.

The uncooked icings are not amateurish cake toppings, they are the soft creams that adorn the French cakes and most of the Torten. They are the icings that made Budapest famous and they are the base out of which all those lovely rosettes and swirls can be made. Fill your next cake with a butter cream, top it with a different cream and press what is left through a pastry tube into arabesques and when necessary into "Happy Birthday." Chill the cake to keep your message from running.

COFFEE-COCOA FROSTING

½ pound butter, creamed
3 cups confectioners sugar
4 tablespoons coffee essence or
    instant coffee powder

4 tablespoons cocoa
1 cup chopped toasted nuts

Add all ingredients, gradually, to creamed butter. Beat frosting until smooth, spread on cake and dust with nuts.

BUTTER CREAM

1 cup butter
1 pound confectioners sugar

½ teaspoon vanilla

Cream butter with sugar and vanilla in electric beater until light. Add vanilla and chill 10 minutes.

Variation:
Coffee Butter Cream: add 3 tablespoons instant coffee to creamed butter.

ORANGE FROSTING

2 3-ounce packages cream cheese
2 tablespoons orange juice

2 teaspoons grated orange rind
4½ cups confectioners sugar

Stir cheese and orange juice until smooth. Gradually add rind and sugar, chill for 20 minutes.

COFFEE CREAM CAKE FROSTING

2 3-ounce packages cream cheese
2 tablespoons heavy cream
1½ tablespoons instant coffee

4¼ cups confectioners sugar
1½ teaspoons vanilla

Combine cheese, cream, coffee and sugar, adding sugar gradually and beating well. Add vanilla and a little more sugar, if needed to obtain best spreading consistency.

BUDAPEST ICING

3 squares chocolate, melted
1½ cups confectioners sugar
2½ tablespoons hot coffee

3 egg yolks
⅓ cup soft butter

Beat chocolate, sugar and coffee together. Add yolks one at a time, beating until each yolk is incorporated. Beat in butter, bit by bit, until icing is of spreading consistency.

CHOCOLATE BUTTER CREAM

3 squares chocolate
⅓ cup soft butter
3 cups confectioners sugar, sifted

¼ cup heavy cream
1 teaspoon vanilla

Melt chocolate over hot water. Cream butter until light. Gradually add sugar, chocolate, cream and vanilla, beating in alternately.

COFFEE BUTTER CREAM

1½ squares chocolate
1 tablespoon instant coffee
⅓ cup soft butter

3 cups confectioners sugar, sifted
¼ cup heavy cream
1½ teaspoon rum

Melt chocolate over hot water. Cream butter until light, gradually add sugar, coffee and cream, beating as each addition is made. Flavor with rum.

CHOCOLATE ICING

1 cup confectioners sugar
2 egg yolks
¼ cup cream
1 teaspoon vanilla

4 squares chocolate, melted over hot water
1 tablespoon soft butter

Beat all ingredients in electric beater until smooth. Chill until proper spreading consistency is reached.

FUDGE ICING

2 packages semi-sweet chocolate bits ¼ cup soft butter
3 cups confectioners sugar, sifted ½ cup hot cream

Melt chocolate over hot water, or in double boiler, add sugar, butter and cream gradually. Beat until icing is smooth and of proper spreading consistency.

SUGAR BUTTER ICING

1 cup four-X sugar   cold water
juice of ½ lemon   ¼ cup creamed butter

Beat sugar and lemon juice with enough water to make a smooth thick cream. Whip in creamed butter and chill 15 minutes. Beat again and spread on commercial cup or layer cakes.

ROYAL BUTTER FOR BAKERY

4 hard-cooked egg yolks   ⅔ cup powdered sugar
⅔ cup butter, creamed   1 teaspoon orange flavor

Rice egg yolks and stir into butter, add sugar and orange flavor. Use to ice prepared cake layers.

CHAPTER 15.   *Confections*

THE making of confections has been classed as an art, perhaps not actually alongside of painting, sculpture and music, but not far behind. The knowledge, ability and dexterity which were needed to fulfill the requirements were known as the "Confectioner's Art." And no wonder . . . the confectioner was expected to create great sugared masterpieces depicting the Eiffel Tower, the Crystal Palace and any architectural monument which was celebrating an anniversary. The confectioner was not only able to build fragile buildings, he could make replicas of coronations, presentations and weddings. He could make cupids and swans and he was able to nest them in clouds of spun sugar. As far as flowers and butterflies were concerned, even the poorest confectioner became a creative artist.

Now we are reduced in many districts to getting our sweetmeats, comfits and dainties out of slot machines or at newsstands and drugstores. The confectionery is an almost forgotten establishment and the confectioner is nearly extinct.

We all know how to make fudge, but there our knowledge ends and, judging by the packaged mixes, it looks as though our children won't even know how to do that. There are chocolate Truffles, mints and confections that require no cooking and will satisfy and delight the sweet teeth we are endowed with.

214

FRUIT NUT SQUARES

½ cup walnuts
½ cup pecans
½ cup figs
½ cup dates

3 pieces candied orange rind
1 tablespoon orange juice
1 large bar milk chocolate, melted

Put first 5 ingredients through food grinder twice to obtain a stiff paste. Add orange juice, and press paste out ½ inch thick on a sugared board. Dribble over milk chocolate, melted over hot water and cut into squares. Press a pecan half onto each square and allow to dry for 1 hour.

APRICOT BULLETS

18 dried apricots
¾ cup shredded coconut
2 teaspoons orange or apricot juice

½ teaspoon vanilla
3 tablespoons confectioners sugar

Put apricots and coconut through meat grinder or food chopper, mix paste with fruit juice and vanilla. Apricot liqueur may be substituted for orange or apricot juice. Shape into marble-sized balls, roll in confectioners sugar and chill for 1 hour.

CREAM FUDGE

1 3-ounce package cream cheese
2 cups confectioners sugar
½ teaspoon vanilla
½ cup chopped almonds

1 pinch salt
2 squares semi-sweet chocolate,
    melted over hot water

Beat or blend all ingredients to a smooth paste. Press into a buttered pan, mark in squares and chill until firm.

FUDGE

4 squares semi-sweet chocolate
1 tablespoon butter
1 well-beaten egg
3 tablespoons heavy cream

1 pinch salt
½ teaspoon vanilla
1 cup chopped pecans

Melt chocolate and butter over hot water, stir and cool. Beat egg in a bowl, add cream, salt, vanilla, melted chocolate and pecans. Stir well. Press into a buttered pan, making candy about ½ inch deep. Cool, cut in squares and chill.

CRYSTALLIZED MINT LEAVES

½ bunch mint
1 egg white, beaten stiff

½ cup granulated sugar
6 drops essence of peppermint

Cut stalks from mint leaves. Wipe large leaves dry, dip in beaten egg white and then in sugar mixed with peppermint essence. Lay leaves on waxed paper and dry in a very slow oven 225° F. Dip a second time and dry again if a heavier coating is desired.

UNCOOKED MINTS

½ pound icing sugar
½ teaspoon peppermint essence
    (can be purchased at any
    drug store)

½ egg white, well beaten

Work sugar and essence with just enough egg white to form a stiff paste. Set aside for 3 hours. Roll out and cut into desired shapes, or drop mixture by teaspoonsful onto waxed paper before its three-hour rest.

MARZIPAN

½ pound blanched almonds,
    ground
2 teaspoons orange or lemon juice
2¼ cups powdered sugar

1 well-beaten egg
few drops orange flower water,
    optional

Grind almonds several times, as finely as possible. Pound with orange or lemon juice and add sugar. Bind with egg, adding only a little at a time and adding very gradually while kneading and working the paste. Roll out the paste and cut or shape as desired.

CINNAMON MARZIPAN

½ recipe Marzipan shaped into
    small balls
1 egg white, beaten

1 teaspoon cinnamon
¼ cup confectioners sugar

Roll marzipan balls in egg white, allow to dry for 15 minutes. Roll in cinnamon mixed with sugar.

TRUFFLES

1 8-ounce can blanched almonds,
    ground
2½ cups icing sugar
3 tablespoons cocoa powder

1 teaspoon coffee essence
1 egg, well beaten
¼ teaspoon almond or vanilla
    essence

Work all ingredients together into a stiff, smooth paste. Roll in balls with hands, dusting palms with sugar and cocoa combined to taste. Set truffles aside for 2 hours. Brush with corn syrup and roll in coconut or chocolate shot or leave plain as preferred.

DATE BALLS

6 marshmallows
1 cup pitted dates
1 cup pecans

¼ cup condensed milk
2 tablespoons powdered sugar
6 graham crackers, crushed

Cut marshmallows into small dice with floured scissors, combine with next 4 ingredients. Form into marbles and roll in cracker crumbs.

BOURBON BALLS

3 cups ground chocolate wafers
1 cup ground pecans
1 cup confectioners sugar

3 tablespoons light corn syrup
½ cup bourbon whiskey
2 tablespoons cocoa

Mix first 5 ingredients and form into marbles. Roll in cocoa and store until needed.

UNCOOKED FONDANT

½ cup confectioners sugar, sieved
¼ teaspoon cream of tartar
1 teaspoon evaporated milk

¼ teaspoon vanilla essence
½ egg white, beaten

Work first 4 ingredients together into a dry paste, add only enough egg white to work into a smooth and pliable paste. Knead well, chill for 1 hour and use to fill nuts, dates, figs or other confections.

FONDANT WALNUTS

48 walnut halves
2 teaspoons grated orange rind
1 teaspoon orange juice

½ cup Uncooked Fondant
1 egg white, beaten
¼ cup confectioners sugar

Knead orange juice and rind into chilled Fondant. Form into 24 little balls, press a walnut half on each side, brush with egg white and roll in sugar.

CHAPTER 16.

Beverages

SOME of these beverages are heated and some are chilled, but none of them call for more skill than it takes to shake or stir a drink.

The fact is that this entire book was inspired by the facility with which certain alcoholic ingredients, properly combined, could produce such really startling results without being cooked, as viz the Martini. All this was then translated into vegetables, eggs and fruit and resulted in a more nourishing, if less inspiring, group of combinations.

In this chapter there are a few recipes that are not, as so many punches are, simply a way of serving drinks to a party without spending too much on them. These punches and Bowlen are memorable in themselves and call for special occasions for their preparation. The entire month of May is such an occasion, as would be any hot summer evening or cold winter night. They are perfect for the kind of special occasions that are bound to occur frequently in all our lives.

ANANAS CHAMPAGNE

½ bottle brandy
1 bottle champagne

1 fresh pineapple
granulated sugar to taste

Cut lid from pineapple, cut out meat, leaving shell intact. Dice pineapple, sugar to taste, pour brandy over and marinate in refrigerator for 2 hours. Refill pineapple with fruit and brandy. Spoon into glasses and fill with iced champagne. Pineapple should be refilled with cold brandied fruit, if shell is too small to hold all of it.

A COOLER SUMMER

2 bottles Moselle wine, iced
1 lemon peel cut from lemon in a
    single spiral curl

2 tablespoons sugar
1 bottle soda, chilled
juice of 1 lemon

Combine all ingredients, chill and serve.

RUSSIAN CHAMPAGNE

juice of 1 lemon
juice of 1 orange

4 jiggers vodka
1 bottle iced champagne

Shake first 3 ingredients with ice, fill glasses half full, add iced champagne to fill glasses.

GLÖG

½ bottle brandy
12 cloves
12 cardamon seeds
¾ cup blanched almonds
1 cup raisins

1 cinnamon stick
¼ cup diced orange peel
1 bottle claret
1 bottle port
½ pound lump sugar

Pour brandy over next 6 ingredients and marinate for 24 hours. Add wines, heat to just under boiling and keep at that temperature for 15 minutes. Place a few lumps of sugar on a slotted spoon over bowl containing Glög. Pour brandy over sugar, light and let sugar drip into bowl as it melts. Repeat until all sugar is used. Serve hot Glög immediately.

MAY WINE

⅔ cup dried or fresh woodruff
2 bottles white wine
1 bottle light red wine
3 tablespoons sugar

1 basket hulled strawberries
½ cup orange juice
1 bottle champagne

Steep woodruff in wine for 30 minutes. Add sugar and strain into chilled punch bowl. Add strawberries, pack bowl in chopped ice and add orange juice and champagne just before serving. (Dried woodruff may be bought at a store. It is the herb that "CURES ALL ILLS.")

BLENDER BANANA
(in electric blender)

1 banana, peeled and quartered
1 tablespoon thin honey

1 cup milk, chilled

Blend 10 seconds and serve to a member of the younger generation.

CENTRAL POWERS

1 bottle Rhine wine
1 bottle champagne

1 bottle Swedish punch

Combine, chill and serve.

STORMY WEATHER

2 lemon rinds
1 bottle light white wine

⅓ cup sugar
1 pint champagne

Place lemon rind in wine and set aside in a cool place for 8 hours. Add sugar and champagne just before serving.

PINEAPPLE BOWL

½ bottle Chablis
1 pineapple, peeled and sliced
⅓ cup sugar
½ bottle port wine

½ bottle sherry
½ bottle Chablis
½ cup curaçao
1 bottle champagne

Pour Chablis over pineapple, add sugar and set aside 30 minutes, add next 3 ingredients at 30-minute intervals. Add curaçao and champagne and serve iced.

PEACH CHAMPAGNE

4 peaches, scalded and peeled
¼ cup or 4 tablespoons brandy

4 splits champagne

Place skinned peaches in 4 tall glasses. Puncture with fork in 8 or 10 places, pour over brandy and set aside for 20 minutes. Add chilled champagne and serve at once.

ROSÉ PEACHES

4 peaches, peeled
⅓ cup sugar

4 ounces rum
1 bottle rosé wine, chilled

Marinate peaches with sugar and rum for 3 hours. Add wine and serve in iced glasses.

THE BISHOP MISBEHAVES

1 bottle claret
¾ cup sugar
¼ teaspoon cinnamon

2 orange rinds—cut with potato parer

Heat all ingredients to boiling and serve at once.

GLOW WINE

2 bottles claret
1¼ cups sugar

½ stick cinnamon
2 cloves

Bring all ingredients to boiling. Stir well and serve at once.

MINTED TEA

¼ cup crushed mint leaves
2 tablespoons sugar
2 teaspoons lemon juice
½ cup strong tea

½ cup bourbon
2 cups shaved ice
4 sprigs mint

Crush mint leaves with sugar and lemon juice. Add tea, bourbon and ice. *Shake* well and serve with a sprig of mint in each beaker.

SLEEPLESS NIGHT

¼ cup instant coffee
2 tablespoons sugar

2 cups cold water
½ cup brandy

Combine all ingredients, shake very well, pour over shaved ice and serve as cold as possible.

TEA SQUARE PUNCH

1 quart strong tea
1½ pints pineapple juice
½ cup lemon juice
1 cup orange juice

½ cup sugar
1 quart ginger ale, chilled
½ cup strawberries, hulled

Mix first 5 ingredients and chill. Just before serving add ginger ale and strawberries and serve at once.

RUM COOLER I

(in electric blender)

4 ounces fresh orange juice
4 ounces fresh lime juice
6 ounces Jamaica rum

2 tablespoons sugar
2 teaspoons grated orange rind
12 fresh raspberries

Place first 4 ingredients in blender with cracked ice. Blend for half a minute. Float raspberries on top, serve in 4 tall glasses, dusted with orange rind.

RUM COOLER II

(in electric blender)

½ cup frozen strawberries with
    their syrup
4 ounces fresh lime juice

8 to 12 fresh strawberries
6 ounces Jamaica rum

Place first 3 ingredients in blender with cracked ice. Blend ½ minute. Serve in large glasses and add fresh strawberries.

AMBROSIA

1 part port wine
1 part brandy

2 parts cold, strong, black coffee
chopped ice

Shake with ice and serve with cheese for breakfast. This is the sort of breakfasts that you are still up for; not the kind you get up for.

DEATH IN WARSAW

2 bottles Burgundy
1 cinnamon stick
yellow outside peel of 1 lemon

2 cloves
1 pound lump sugar, large lumps
rum

Heat Burgundy with cinnamon, lemon peel and cloves, but do not let it boil. Pour into a metal punch bowl, lay a wire mesh across the bowl. (The Poles crossed their swords across the bowl, but enough of that.) Mound the lump sugar on the mesh. Saturate it with as much rum as it will absorb. Light the rum (turn out the lights in the room, of course, so that Death in Warsaw may be enjoyable) and allow the melting sugar to drip through the mesh (or swords) into the bowl. As soon as the flame dies down, drink.

A small refrigerator tray makes a good mesh. Do not use anything as fine as screening, as the sugar will not run through.

PORT WINE BOWL

To one pint basket of large juicy blackberries, add 1 bottle port and 1 bottle red wine. Let berries marinate in wine for 1 hour, add 1 bottle of champagne and serve. Put a few berries into each glass of punch served.

FOGGY FOGGY DEW

2 cups sweet red wine
2 bottles red Bordeaux wine
1 pint soda water

8 peaches
1 bottle champagne

Pour chilled wines and soda water into a punch bowl, packed in chopped ice. Dip peaches in boiling water, draw off skins and slice into the bowl. Crack peach pits, with a nut cracker, extract almonds, pull off the skins and add to bowl. Just before serving add 1 bottle iced champagne.

WHISKEY SOUR

3 parts blended whiskey
2 parts lemon juice

1 part granulated sugar
heavy rum

Shake first 3 ingredients very well with lots of ice. Pour into whiskey sour glasses and float a half teaspoon rum on each glass.

CHOCOLATE DROPS

3 cups cold chocolate
1½ cups strong cold coffee
½ cup brandy

3 tablespoons sugar
⅔ cup whipped cream

Combine all ingredients and serve.

ARTILLERY PUNCH

1 bottle rye whiskey
1 bottle brandy

1 bottle claret
1 bottle sherry

Combine, ice and serve.

GESPRITZTER

Add chilled soda water to chilled white wine in a tall glass. Proper proportion is half wine, half soda.

EGG NOG I

1 egg
4 tablespoons bourbon (1 jigger)
2 teaspoons powdered sugar

1 cup light cream
1 grating nutmeg

Shake well with ice, serve topped with nutmeg.

EGG NOG II

6 egg yolks
¾ cup powdered sugar
½ bottle rum
3 cups milk

2 cups heavy cream
6 egg whites beaten stiff
nutmeg

Beat egg yolks and sugar until light. Gradually beat in rum, milk and cream. Fold in egg whites, dust with nutmeg and serve very cold.

BLACK BEAUTY

(in electric blender)

2 cups chocolate ice cream   ¼ cup walnuts
½ cup crème de cacao

Combine ice cream and liqueur in blender until smooth. Add nuts and serve.

BLOODY MARY

2 cups tomato juice   ¼ teaspoon pepper
1½ cups vodka   juice of 3 lemons
3 dashes Worcestershire sauce   ¼ teaspoon salt
1 dash Tobasco Sauce

Shake well with lots of ice and serve, especially on a late Sunday morning.

KEEP COOL

(in electric blender)

4 tablespoons Triple Sec (1 jigger)   1 teaspoon sugar
⅓ cup orange juice   ½ cup shaved ice
1½ tablespoons lemon juice

Blend in electric blender. Serve in wide cocktail glasses with straws.

BLENDED EGGS

2 cups tomato juice   1 tablespoon chives
2 eggs

Blend eggs with hot or cold tomato juice, dust with chives and serve.

ER LIEBT MICH VOM HERZEN
(He Loves Me)

½ cup brandy
½ cup port wine
3 tablespoons sugar

4 egg yolks
2 tablespoons chopped or grated
    filberts or hazel nuts

Chill all ingredients. Shake very well with lots of ice, and serve at once.

CHAPTER 17.   # Rice
                               and
                               Pastas

S INCE we are even more determined than you are that you shall not cook, the recipes in this chapter are based on canned wild rice, canned spaghetti, macaroni and ravioli and on canned or cooked white rice. Regarding the white rice, it is assumed that if you are using this book because you are no cook at all you may still make Minute Rice, or if you are a cook that you will have cooked rice in the refrigerator, or that you are using canned rice.

In any case, *the following measurements are important.* One fourteen-ounce can wild rice, drained, measures 1½ cups of rice and better than ¾ cup liquid. In following the recipes, it is necessary to add some moisture to rice which is dry and fluffy, but less moisture to canned rice which comes packed in its own liquid and retains a good deal of moisture even after it is drained. It is also important to remember that no matter how well drained a can of tomatoes may be, it will still add liquid to the recipe. Cold rice and macaroni salads are in the salad chapter and for a NO COOKING cook who just by chance may have a box of medium-fine, cooked hot noodles on her hands, we suggest:

Stir them with ¼ pound butter and 1 cup grated Parmesan cheese. Stir them in a chafing dish or on a hot platter or keep the platter on a warming tray while you stir. Season to taste and give it a few grindings from your rough-grinding pepper mill. If you want to take this a step further, be sure the pepper corns in the pepper mill are Tellicherry pepper and after that you can rest content, there is nothing more you can do to improve your Fettuccini Alfredo except eat them. To stay in the spirit of this book, we can only hope your neighbor will suddenly give you some hot cooked noodles or that you'll come across them unexpectedly— so far no one has put them up in a jar.

If you do not want to turn on the oven, all these heat-and-serve recipes may be prepared in the upper section of a double boiler over boiling water or in a chafing dish.

RAVIOLI ALFREDO

To two 15½-ounce cans ravioli in tomato sauce, add 1 can sliced mushrooms, ½ crushed garlic clove, ¼ cup chopped parsley and ¼ cup each chopped green pepper and chopped onion. Heat according to directions on the can and pass grated Parmesan cheese separately. Serve with a spinach salad.

FRENCH RICE

2 cups cooked or canned rice
1 11-ounce jar boned chicken
½ lemon, juice and grated rind
½ cup roughly chopped walnuts

1 buffet-size can small white
    cocktail onions with liquor
1 pinch of thyme
2 teaspoons toasted sesame seeds
salt and pepper

Combine all ingredients including the aspic jelly around the chicken and heat to boiling in a buttered casserole in a moderately hot 375° F oven. Serve with a water cress or spinach salad and toasted French bread.

SPANISH RICE

1 cup peeled and cubed bologna
    sausage
1 clove garlic, crushed
1 buffet-size can small white
    onions, drained
1 green pepper, seeded and
    chopped
1 8-ounce can tomatoes, drained

3 cups cooked or canned rice
¼ cup chopped parsley
½ cup beef broth
12 stuffed olives, sliced
1 pinch saffron
grated rind of 1 orange
salt and pepper to taste

Heat all ingredients to boiling in a buttered casserole in a moderately hot 375° F oven. Serve with salad and garlic bread.

ITALIAN RICE

1 cup diced ham
¼ cup chopped chives
1 cup chopped onion
½ cup chopped green pepper
1 8-ounce can tomatoes, drained
3 cups cooked or canned rice

1 can cream of mushroom soup
½ teaspoon oregano or to taste
½ teaspoon thyme or to taste
salt and pepper
1 cup grated Parmesan cheese

Combine first 9 ingredients in a buttered baking dish, season to taste and heat through in a moderately hot oven 375° F. Serve with a green salad and pass Parmesan separately.

AVOCADO RICE

2 cups cooked or canned rice
3 tablespoons chicken consommé
½ teaspoon marjoram or to taste
⅓ cup finely minced parsley
salt and pepper

2 teaspoons lemon juice
½ teaspoon grated lemon rind
2 avocados, peeled, seeded and
    diced
freshly ground black pepper

Heat first 7 ingredients through in a casserole in a moderately hot oven 375° F. Just before serving, stir in the diced avocado and sprinkle with freshly ground pepper.

Serve with broiled chicken or lamb steaks or chops, or add 2 cups cubed, cooked chicken and serve as a main dish.

PINEAPPLE RICE

3 cups cooked or canned rice
1 can pineapple chunks, drained
½ green pepper, seeded and
   minced

¼ can chicken consommé
salt and pepper
1 avocado, peeled, seeded and
   diced

Heat rice, pineapple chunks, green pepper and consommé in a buttered casserole to boiling, add a little of the juice from pineapple and season to taste. Just before serving, sprinkle with avocado dice and a little more salt and pepper. Serve with lamb.

RISI PISI

3 cups cooked or canned rice
1 8-ounce can peas
3 tablespoons broth

salt and white pepper
2 tablespoons butter

Combine first 3 ingredients in a baking dish, season to taste and heat to boiling in a moderately hot 375° F oven.

Just before serving, stir in the butter. Serve with fried chicken, breaded cutlets or chicken and veal roast.

SPAGHETTI WITH SHRIMPS

2 15½-ounce cans spaghetti in
   mushroom sauce
1 can shrimps
½ cup grated cheese

½ green pepper, seeded and finely
   chopped
½ teaspoon oregano
salt and pepper

½ cup grated cheese

Combine first 6 ingredients in a buttered baking dish. Heat through in a moderately hot 375° F oven and serve with a mixed green salad. Pass grated cheese separately.

MACARONI SALMON CASSEROLE

2 15½-ounce cans macaroni in
    cheese sauce
1 1-pound can salmon, flaked
½ cup heavy cream

1 pimiento, diced
salt and pepper
3 tablespoons chopped parsley
3 tablespoons grated cheese

Combine first 4 ingredients in a buttered casserole, season to taste and sprinkle top with parsley and cheese. Heat in a moderately hot 375° F oven. Serve with a green salad. Spaghetti in cheese sauce may be substituted for the macaroni.

RICE AND SHRIMP CASSEROLE

3 cups cooked or canned rice
½ can tomato soup
1 8-ounce can cooked green peas
1 can shrimps
1 cup grated American cheese

½ teaspoon dried or fresh chopped
    dill
1 pinch thyme
salt and pepper
¼ cup chopped parsley

Combine rice with next 6 ingredients in a buttered casserole, season to taste and heat to boiling in a moderately hot 375° F oven. Stir well, sprinkle with parsley and serve.

    Increase amount of tomato soup if a moister rice is preferred.

CURRIED RICE

3 cups cooked or canned white rice
¼ cup chicken consommé
2 tomatoes, peeled, seeded and
    chopped or ½ cup canned
    tomatoes, drained

½ cup chopped onion
2 tablespoons soft butter
1 teaspoon curry powder
salt and pepper

Combine first 4 ingredients in a casserole and heat to boiling in a moderately hot 375° F oven. Stir butter and curry powder into a smooth paste, stir the paste into the rice and season to taste. Serve the rice with any meat or poultry and pass chutney separately.

CHUTNEY

¼ pound pitted dates
¼ pound dried apricots
1 cup vinegar
1 hot chili pepper, minced
½ cup sugar, or to taste

½ cup peeled, chopped apple
2 chopped onions
¼ teaspoon ground cinnamon
¼ teaspoon ground ginger
¼ teaspoon ground cloves

Soak dates and apricots in vinegar overnight. Chop finely, add the pepper, apple and onions and the 3 spices. Add a little vinegar if necessary and set aside for 1 hour. Serve with curried rice. This chutney may be put through the meat grinder if preferred.

HERBED SPAGHETTI OR RAVIOLI

¾ cup parsley sprigs
¼ cup basil sprigs
2 sprigs oregano
1 cup walnut meats
2 cloves garlic, crushed
1 cup grated Parmesan

salt and freshly ground black
    pepper
½ cup olive oil
2 cans cooked spaghetti or ravioli
    without sauce

Blend or grind first 7 ingredients. If a blender is used, turn it on only long enough to chop fine, but not to pulverize. Add olive oil gradually, stirring well until sauce has desired consistency. Heat spaghetti or ravioli according to directions on can and mix with herb sauce. If fresh herbs are not available, use 1 cup parsley and 1 teaspoon dried oregano and basil.

ALMOND RICE

3 cups cooked or canned rice
1 cup blanched, slivered almonds
2 cans beef stew
12 stuffed green olives, chopped
½ green pepper, seeded and
    chopped
1 onion, finely chopped
½ garlic clove, crushed

½ cup small raisins
1 tomato, peeled, seeded and
    chopped
½ teaspoon oregano
1 bay leaf
salt and pepper
3 tablespoons chopped parsley

Combine first 11 ingredients in a casserole, season to taste and heat to boiling in a moderately hot 375° F oven. Serve very hot with parsley sprinkled on the top. Serve with any salad or vegetable dish; very good with endive salad or Chiffonade Salad.

WILD RICE

2 14-ounce cans wild rice
¼ cup of liquid drained from rice
¼ cup chopped onion
2 tablespoons chopped green
    pepper

2 tablespoons toasted sesame seeds
2 tablespoons butter
salt and pepper

Toasted sesame seeds can now be purchased at any herb and spice counter. Heat first 5 ingredients to boiling in a moderately hot 375° F oven, in a casserole. Stir in butter and season to taste. Serve with any meat, chicken or game bird.

WILD RICE WITH MUSHROOMS

½ can cream of mushroom soup
2 14-ounce cans wild rice
½ lemon, juice only

1 6-ounce can small button
    mushrooms, drained
2 tablespoons sherry, or to taste
salt and pepper

Heat all ingredients to boiling in a buttered casserole in a moderately hot 375° F oven. Serve with meat, game or any birds. Add 2 cups diced, left-over meat to the casserole and make it into a main course. Serve with a green salad.

WILD RICE AND ARTICHOKES

¼ cup chicken consommé
1 8-ounce can hearts of artichoke,
    drained
2 14-ounce cans wild rice, drained
½ teaspoon marjoram

½ teaspoon thyme
salt and pepper
2 tablespoons minced parsley
1 tablespoon butter

Heat consommé, artichoke hearts, rice and herbs in a casserole in a moderately hot oven 375° F. Season to taste and just before serving, stir in parsley and butter. Serve with lamb steaks, roast or lamb chops. If you really like wild rice, you can serve it with any meat or bird.

WILD RICE AND OYSTERS

1 pint oysters with their liquor
2 14-ounce cans wild rice, drained
1 small onion, minced
¼ cup finely chopped green
    pepper
3 tablespoons finely chopped
    parsley

1 4-ounce can chopped mushrooms,
    drained
salt and freshly ground black
    pepper

Drain oysters and combine them with all other ingredients in a buttered casserole. Season to taste and add just enough of the oyster liquor to moisten, not more than ¼ cup. Heat in a moderately hot 375° F oven and serve very hot with chicken or game birds, but it is especially good with duck.

WILD RICE WITH ONIONS

2 14-ounce cans wild rice, drained
¼ cup beef broth
2 cans, buffet size, small white
    onions, drained (2 cups)
¼ cup chopped chives

½ cup finely chopped celery
salt and pepper
1 tablespoon butter
¼ cup pine nuts, optional

Combine first 5 ingredients in a baking dish. Season to taste and heat through in a moderately hot 375° F oven. Just before serving, stir in butter and serve with any meat or bird; very good with cornish game hens or pheasant.

WILD RICE AND CRAB MEAT

2 14-ounce cans wild rice
1 bottle cocktail onions, drained
½ green pepper, seeded and finely
  chopped
½ bay leaf
½ clove garlic, crushed

3 tablespoons chopped parsley
1 5-ounce can crab meat, picked
  and flaked
½ cup heavy cream
salt and pepper
4 hard-cooked eggs, sliced

Drain liquid from rice and set it aside. Combine rice with next 6 ingredients in a buttered casserole and season to taste. Add a little of the liquid from rice to moisten, not more than ¼ cup, and heat in a moderately hot 375° F oven. Just before serving, stir the cream into the casserole, take out bay leaf and cover with the hard-cooked egg slices. Heat a few minutes longer and serve with a cucumber or green salad.

MACARONI OR SPAGHETTI IN CHEESE SAUCE

2 15½-ounce cans macaroni or
  spaghetti in cheese sauce
1 8-ounce can tomatoes, drained
½ cup chopped stuffed olives
1 onion, chopped

salt and pepper to taste
8-ounce container shredded
  American cheese

Combine first 5 ingredients in a baking dish, top with shredded cheese and heat through in a moderately hot 375° F oven.

SPAGHETTI OR MACARONI IN HERB SAUCE
(Heat to Boiling and Serve)

¾ cup parsley sprigs
¼ cup basil sprigs
2 sprigs oregano
1 cup walnut meats
2 cloves garlic, crushed
1 cup grated Parmesan

salt and freshly ground black
  pepper
½ cup olive oil
2 cans cooked spaghetti or macaroni
  without sauce

Blend or grind first 7 ingredients. If a blender is used, turn it on only long enough to chop fine, but not to pulverize. Add olive oil gradually, stirring well until sauce has desired consistency. Heat spaghetti or macaroni according to directions on can and mix with herb sauce. If fresh herbs are not available, use 1 cup parsley and 1 teaspoon dried oregano and basil.

SPAGHETTI HAM CASSEROLE

½ cup chopped ham
¼ cup chopped onion
1 6-ounce can chopped mushrooms
2 15½-ounce cans spaghetti in
   tomato sauce

salt and pepper to taste
½ teaspoon paprika
½ cup Parmesan cheese
½ cup dry bread crumbs
Parmesan cheese

Combine first 6 ingredients in a buttered baking dish. Top with mixed cheese and crumbs and heat through in a moderately hot 370° F oven. Pass additional Parmesan cheese separately.

NEAR EAST RICE

2 cups cooked or canned rice
1 11-ounce can boned chicken,
   cubed
1 1-pound can tomatoes, drained
1 1-pound jar sliced okra, drained
1 tablespoon sugar

1 teaspoon salt
1 pimiento, chopped
½ green pepper, chopped
1 onion, chopped
⅓ cup chopped mixed herbs or ⅓
   cup chopped parsley

Combine all ingredients, correct seasoning and heat in a buttered casserole in a moderately hot 375° F oven. Cold left-over lamb or veal can be substituted for the chicken.

Index